# *Kids Dine Out*

A
**&RESTAURANTS**
**&INSTITUTIONS**
BOOK

# Kids Dine Out

## *Attracting the Family Foodservice Market with Children's Menus and Pint-Sized Promotions*

### SUSAN GILLERAN

**John Wiley & Sons, Inc.**
*New York / Chichester / Brisbane /
Toronto / Singapore*

Restaurants & Institutions books—co-sponsored by John Wiley & Sons, Inc., and Restaurants & Institutions magazine—are designed to help foodservice professionals build stronger operations.

ISBN 0-471-57500-3

Printed in the United States of America

10 9 8 7 6 5 4 3 2 1

# Contents

# *Foreword*

During the 1950s I had my first eating-out experience: monthly family dinners at which my parents, aunts and uncles, and my 80-year-old Irish grandmother enjoyed the ritual of fine dining. I remember the thick white tablecloths, the silver trays with candied hors d'oeuvres, the wine being opened with expert twists, and the ordering of sophisticated little after-dinner drinks with curious names. Being allowed to share in this dining experience made me feel very adult. In fact, 40 years ago restaurants featured one kind of food—grown-up food. Kids were forced to eat it or go hungry.

Children of the 1980s and 1990s have it much better. In fact, the restaurant world turns progressively on making them happy. Quick-service giants cater to their trendy whims. Former singles-oriented dinnerhouse chains do cartwheels to please parents with kids. Even fine-dining establishments now have a supply of booster seats for little guests.

Successful restaurant marketing at almost any level means knowing how to reach kids and, through them, their parents. When I first heard that Susan Gilleran wanted to do a book on "kids' dining," I said, "Great idea!" Since the 1980s *Restaurants and Institutions* has been running stories on the new generation of food-service customers. We have learned they are smart, clear about what they want from service people, often adventurous in menu choices, and totally tuned in to the eating-out experience. These are MTV, interactive-computer, touch-tone people who want it all at a good price in the right environment when they want it, which was five minutes before they hit the door.

If you haven't figured out that kids are your present and future, then read this book. It's written by the quintessential 1990s mom—full-time professional writer, mother of three, faced with all the pressures today's parents face. One way parents today deal with these challenges is by eating out on a regular basis. The restaurant that knows how to market to them, deliver on its promises, and keep them coming back is a winner.

Gilleran gives you the numbers, the techniques, the suppliers, and the ideas that will get you up and running on the "kidtrack." If you aren't running with the kids, they'll run right over you—or in the other direction.

Michael Bartlett
Editor-in-Chief
*Restaurants & Institutions*

# *Preface*

Every parent likes to think his or her child is unique. But by all reports, my three young children speak for every kid dining out. They get impatient waiting for food to be served. Then, as soon as the food arrives, they have to use the rest rooms. Once they're finished eating, they can't wait to leave.

Sitting at counters immediately sends them into tailspins. Sitting in booths, they tend to adopt the party sitting in the booth directly behind them. They fidget. They kick. They bounce. They turn around and stare. Before long, they disappear under the table.

They spill. They play with food, especially spaghetti. They seek escape routes from high chairs. They lose control with catsup bottles.

Looking on the brighter side, children get hungry and must be fed at least three times a day. Because they never dine out alone and exert tremendous influence on a family's decision about where and what to eat, they represent an increasingly influential segment of the dining-out market. The rise in birth rates, single-parent households, and women entering the labor force are additional factors linking the future of foodservice to satisfying future generations.

Obviously, children are too important to ignore. But what does it take to attract the family foodservice trade? After interviewing 65 operators, promotion experts, and menu planners and making my own assessments (as one of 4.8 million working mothers doing my fair share to support the industry), I gathered enough information on the subject to fill a book.

It's now in your hands.

*Kids Dine Out* is designed to give you great ideas for developing

children's menus, promotions, and programs—ideas that will work
for you. It's a foodservice survival guide for the 1990s, based on the
successes of operators across the United States. It will help you cope
with the special needs of families by showing you how others have
tapped into the family market and how you can too. Discover:

- What the young prefer to eat, what parents like them to eat,
  and what is actually being offered.
- What premiums work and why.
- Trends in the packaging of kids' meals.
- Trends in kids' clubs.
- Ways to train your staff to be kid-friendly.
- Where to purchase kid-related merchandise.

Finally, find out how to create a win-win scenario: Your dining
room is bustling with family business. Children are behaving. Parents are beaming. And you've gained a base of loyal, repeat customers.

# *Acknowledgments*

In putting together this book, I would like to thank my family—Gary, Eli, Adrienne, and Gabriel—for forgoing so many nights of home-cooked meals to let me work.

I'd also like to extend deep appreciation to my associates at *Restaurants & Institutions*, especially Steven Mayer, for enabling me to hold down a job and, at the same time, take care of the homefront for all these years.

Without the patience and persistence of Claire Thompson at John Wiley & Sons, Inc., this book would never have come about.

Nor would this book have been possible without the assistance of the operators featured on the following pages. I am indebted to all those who willingly shared their stories and shed so much light on the subject. I also commend them for their efforts and displays of sensitivity to the needs of children and families today.

Bob Vick, vice president of Lettuce Entertain You Productions, Inc., Chicago, will be forever in my favor for enabling us to shoot the cover photo at Bub City Crabshack & Bar-B-Q.

Finally, I'd like to dedicate *Kids Dine Out* to the original working mother, Pearl Leinoff.

# Kids Dine Out

# Chapter One

# *Coming of Age in the 1990s*

In today's dining-out industry, courting kids is one way to gain a competitive advantage. Though it may not be all child's play, the extra effort is definitely worth it when you consider the advantages inherent in pleasing parents and, in the long term, securing a future customer base.

Given the current population trends, children can be expected to be seen and (given their basic nature) heard in restaurants with increasing frequency throughout this decade and into the next millennium. In fact, as the pitter-patter of little feet pounds ever louder—in 41 million U.S. households now headed by baby boomers—family life will continue to dominate consumer spending patterns for some time to come.

The demographic numbers paint a rosy future for foodservice operators catering to families. In the boom-boom years of the 1980s American productivity—in the baby manufacturing department—reached a 20-year high. Over 4 million births were recorded in 1989. The birth rates for 1990 and 1991 were equally impressive, at 4,179,000 and 4,111,000 respectively.

Obviously, the rise in births translates into a growth spurt of youths and teens in the years to come. Flashing forward to the year 2000, the U.S. Census Bureau estimates that the number of children under 18 will swell to over 62 million. Their parents, the 81 million boomers born between 1946 and 1965, will be at their peak professionally and financially, with discretionary dollars destined to flood the economy.

The size and projected scope of the market are all the more impressive when teamed with two other facts of modern life. Today's youth, who currently comprise 26 percent of the population and account for 20 percent of all restaurant visits, are vested consumers sitting on potential gold mines. In addition, they exert tremendous influence on what their parents purchase.

Translated into monetary terms, children's total annual income is estimated at $14 billion, according to James McNeal, professor of marketing at Texas A&M University and the author of several books on marketing to children.

"Actually, James McNeal is understating children's income level," said Watts Wacker, executive vice president of Yankelovich Clancy Shulman, Westport, Connecticut. The Yankelovich/Nickelodeon Youth Monitor Study™, which has been tracking what kids six to 17 years old buy and why since 1987, puts the figure closer to $33 billion. "That's $17 per kid per week in America.

"Children's single largest source of income is from gifts, followed by allowance and money earned from jobs," Wacker added.

Whether the funds come from parents, grandparents, or employers, the food industry is the greatest beneficiary of kids' spending sprees. The two researchers agree that food purchased from both foodservice and retail outlets consume the greatest proportion of kids' dollars. Kids also influence food purchases more than any other category of consumer goods.

According to McNeal's findings, children have a strong say in approximately $146 billion-worth of purchasing decisions. (Again, that's a conservative estimate.) An appetizing $84 billion of that total, or 58 percent, represents food purchases rung up at both foodservice and food retail operations.

"Children are demanding by nature. They make requests, suggestions, appeals, many of which have to do with eating because it's their second favorite pastime, next to play," he said.

## THE MONEY MANIPULATORS

In its study, *The Market for Children and Family Dining*, the National Restaurant Association (NRA) concludes that "Without a doubt, children influence where their family dines."

- In an NRA Gallup survey, of those adults polled more than half (55%) responded positively that their children ages six to 12 are very or somewhat influential in deciding to dine out at a tableservice restaurant. What's more, nearly half (47%) agreed that their children six to 12 are fairly influential in determining which tableservice restaurant to eat at. (See Figure 1–1.)
- Even children six and younger have a say. According to the survey, 48 percent of adults rated children under six as being fairly influential in the decision to eat out, and 45 percent admitted that children under six have a say in deciding where to eat. (See Figure 1–2.)

To dine out or not to dine out? And where shall we go? These are questions that approximately half of all parents reported leaving up to their six- to 12-year-old children.

| | Children Ages 6 to 12 | |
| | Whether to Eat Out | Where to Eat |
|---|---|---|
| 5–Very Influential | 32% | 28% |
| 4 | 23% | 19% |
| 3 | 27% | 24% |
| 2 | 8% | 14% |
| 1–Not At All Influential | 10% | 15% |
| Total | 100% | 100% |

*Source:* National Restaurant Association Gallup Survey, 1990.

Figure 1-1   Children Influence Dining Decisions

Not only do older offspring cast the deciding vote on when to dine and which tableservice restaurant to frequent, the littlest siblings also have a big impact.

| | Children Less than Age 6 | |
| | Whether to Eat Out | Where to Eat |
| --- | --- | --- |
| 5–Very Influential | 35% | 32% |
| 4 | 13% | 13% |
| 3 | 21% | 14% |
| 2 | 8% | 11% |
| 1–Not At All Influential | 23% | 30% |
| Total | 100% | 100% |

*Source:* National Restaurant Association Gallup Survey, 1990.

Figure 1-2   **Young Children Get into the Act**

- Meanwhile, more than three-fourths (78 percent) of all parents with children between seven and 17 years of age credited their offspring with making the family's fast food choice. The same study conducted by the Roper Organization found that 42 percent of parents with kids between seven and 12 and 54 percent of parents with kids 13 to 17 perceived their children as being the household experts on fast food.

## THE FAMILY REVISITED

After studying children's consumer behavior for more than 25 years, McNeal is convinced that their influence on purchases, including dining-out decisions, is a 1980s phenomenon resulting from changes in basic family structure.

"Children's influence has changed enormously in the last few years," said Clifford Scott, another expert on child money matters and president of the marketing consultant firm, The Scott Group, Studio City, California. "The single most important factor accounting for this change is the lack of a full-time parent."

- Due to the high divorce rate and increased incidence of out-of-wedlock births, the number of single-parent families advanced from 6.1 million in 1980 to 7.9 million in 1990—a 28 percent jump. Still, it is important to note that single-parent families are in the minority. "Only 23 percent of boomer households with children are headed by single parents, and nearly 90 percent of these are headed by women," according to *American Demographics*.

- The Bureau of Labor Statistics reports that more than half (nearly 54 percent) of all women 16 and over with children under age three now work outside the home compared to only 34 percent some 15 years ago. (See Figure 1–3.)

- Approximately two-thirds of these women (69%), whose ranks have swelled to 4.8 million, hold full-time jobs.

In attempting to advance careers, take care of kids, and maintain a relationship with a spouse or significant other, baby boomers are caught up in a rat race with no finish line in sight. As pressure mounts for parents to succeed while being pulled in several different directions at once, it stands to reason that those tugging on the heartstrings garner special consideration.

"The net result is a life guided by guilt," said Scott. "Why are kids having so much influence on decisions? It's guilt. Parents don't want to deny them."

Guilt marketing is a concept familiar to Wacker as well. "There has never been an easier time for a kid to get Kool-Aid with dinner," he said. "Over 50 percent of mothers will give kids things that are bad for them—even though they know it."

Another way to explain what Wacker refers to as the "Alexander the Great Phenomenon," which elevates kids to conquerers and central decision-makers, is time—or lack of it.

"We're in a time famine today," Scott added. "It's harder (more time-consuming) to say no."

With both parents working outside the home in three-fourths of all households with children, the evening meal is often the only time to get together, share daily news, bond. Someone has to be in

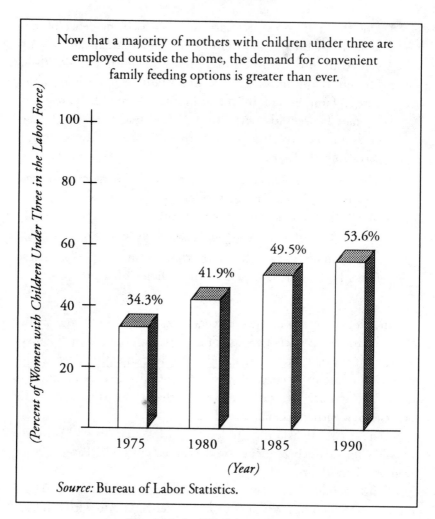

Now that a majority of mothers with children under three are employed outside the home, the demand for convenient family feeding options is greater than ever.

Figure 1-3   Working Women

charge of determining what—and where—to eat. If parents are too busy making money to figure out how to spend it, let the littlest voices in the family pitch in with opinions.

Said McNeal, "Time matters are putting a great deal of pressure on the parent-child relationship. When the family finally has time to spend together, they try to make it special." Often, that translates into acquiescing to children's heartfelt pleas or sugar-coated threats.

McNeal cited two additional reasons why parents yield the power to decide to children in his latest work, *Kids as Customers* (Lexington Books, New York, 1992). He writes, "Parents are having fewer children and therefore tend to give each child more things and more say-so in buying things." Another point: "Having children is often postponed until later in life when parents' careers are established and nest eggs built. When children do arrive, they are given much more attention. Part of this attention is in the form of letting the children join in with mom and dad when planning purchases."

## MEET TODAY'S KID CUSTOMERS

With increasing amounts of time on their hands, on their own, unsupervised by parents, the current generation is significantly different from the baby boomers who came of age in decades past.

"Children are no longer shielded as much as they used to be from life's realities. Their window onto the world is television, which they spend more time on than anything else, other than sleeping. Put together the fact that they don't have the classic mom at home, and are responsible for more of the household chores. And the result is a sophisticated little consumer," Scott said.

"Today's eight-year-old is not the same eight-year-old child of 30 years ago," he stressed. "He or she is smarter, more worldly, and more independent. To better understand who today's children are, I counsel all my clients to add two to three years to actual ages."

In her bestselling *The Popcorn Report* (Doubleday, New York, 1991), trend forecaster Faith Popcorn writes, "Today's weaned-on-television kids have been imprinted at an early impressionable age. They're the latchkey kids who come home from school to an empty house and have to do the shopping: for detergents, dog foods, and frozen dinners. They're coupon-clippers and brand-name conscious.

Think of the boy in the movie *Home Alone*, and how he bugged the checkout woman to find out if his choice of toothbrush was approved by the American Dental Association. Kids today know the right questions to ask."

Watts Wacker of Yankelovich Clancy Shulman, who coins the term "millennium generation" to refer to children who will come of age by the year 2000, agrees that kids today are not the same kids their parents were. It's just not possible. Changing social and cultural conditions are reshaping young lives.

"The millennium generation is very focused," he said. In spite of spending less time with parents and undergoing greater peer and societal pressures, this is a generation that feels able to cope. They believe they will go to college. They believe jobs will be waiting for them as soon as they've completed their education, and that as far as career paths go, there are no male and female stereotypes.

"This is a generation that feels very self-empowered. They are very savvy and sophisticated," Wacker stressed. "They are very talented at getting what they want."

## WHAT DO KIDS REALLY WANT FROM A RESTAURANT?

When dealing with the young, old ways of doing business may no longer apply. For the fact of the matter is, when kid consumers dine out, they demand more than good food or value for their money.

Kids just want to be kids when they accompany parents—or insist on parents accompanying them—to restaurants, according to Wacker. "They want to be placed in situations where they are not going to disturb other people."

A real drawing card for youth is an eating establishment that provides them with a "sense of ownership," interjected Scott. Kids' clubs, menus, placemats, coloring sheets and crayons, a playground or playroom make them feel like the restaurant is theirs.

"Sense of speed" is another irresistible attribute. "Children's attention spans are very short," Scott said. "They want to get in, eat, and get out as fast as they can."

## PREFERRED DINING CHOICES

Not surprisingly, fast food operations fit the bill for the majority of families with children. They offer speedy service, efficiency, convenience, promotions with play value, and the foods kids love at prices parents prefer paying. Indeed, in a study by CREST (Consumer Reports on Eating Share Trends) conducted for the NRA, a walloping 79 percent of households with children under 13 wound up at quickservice restaurants. (See Figure 1–4.) Equally unsurprising, pizza, hamburger, Mexican, and ice cream restaurants were the

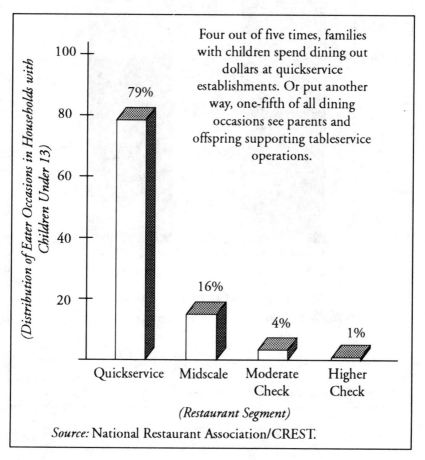

Figure 1-4   Family Dining Habits

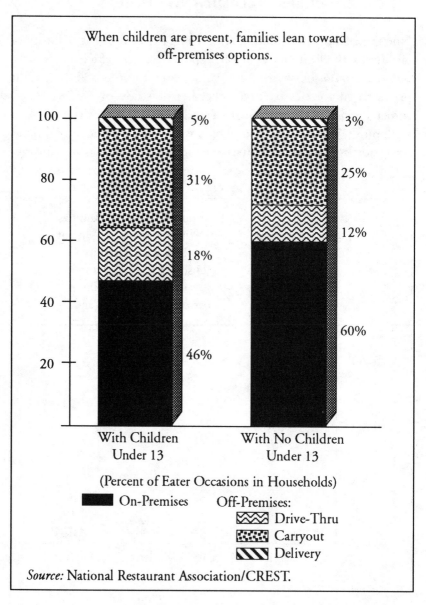

When children are present, families lean toward off-premises options.

With Children Under 13: On-Premises 46%, Drive-Thru 18%, Carryout 31%, Delivery 5%

With No Children Under 13: On-Premises 60%, Drive-Thru 12%, Carryout 25%, Delivery 3%

(Percent of Eater Occasions in Households)

On-Premises   Off-Premises: Drive-Thru, Carryout, Delivery

Source: National Restaurant Association/CREST.

Figure 1-5   Take It Away

types of operations frequented most by households with children under 13.

The presence of children is also driving demand for takeout and delivery. CREST found that in households with children under 13, 54 percent of eater occasions were off-premises compared to 40 percent in households with no children under 13. (See Figure 1–5.)

The NRA confirms the popularity of off-premises eating in its study, *Dinner Decision Making*. When adult respondents were asked why they ordered delivery or carryout, they cited the following family-focused reasons:

- kids' preferences
- convenience
- speed of service
- value for the money

## WHAT DO PARENTS REALLY WANT?

Not to downplay the popularity of on- and off-premises quickservice operations, but aging baby boomers, who grew up on fast food, are showing signs of having had their fill of standing in line, ordering over the counter, consuming a steady diet of pick-up and pop-in-your-mouth food. This may explain why moderately priced, casual eateries featuring a come-as-you-are atmosphere, a more adventurous menu, and such amenities as "being waited on" are also flourishing with families. Approximately one-fifth of all eater occasions in households with children under 13 are at tableservice restaurants. Furthermore, when baby boomer heads of households do venture into the tableservice arena, seven times out of 10 they do so with their entire brood in tow. "So you can't ignore the children if you plan to have their parents as customers," according to the NRA's *The Market for Children and Family Dining*.

The price of going after this market is being able to comply with customers' demands. First and foremost, it's being prepared to satisfy children's appetites.

"One of the most important criteria for parents in choosing a tableservice restaurant is that the establishment offer their children's favorite foods," according to the NRA's survey. Nearly eight out of 10 parents with children younger than 13 rated this factor as being important in their choice of restaurant. Considering that hamburgers and french fries top the list of young children's favorite foods (for more on the subject, see Chapter 3), happy children are obviously more important than healthy cuisine.

Speed of service, child-sized menu portions at lower prices, and reduced-price promotions for children are other amenities of importance to more than half of the parents surveyed. High chairs and diversions such as puzzles or games on menus and coloring books are of greater interest to parents with children younger than six than they are to parents with children between the ages of six and 12.

## TWO SIDES TO THE STORY

Perhaps the best way to put all these facts and figures into perspective and recognize how they impact your business is to play out the following scenario.

Imagine that night is falling. Traffic is heading home.

After putting in eight or more hours at work, dad and/or mom convene with the kids, who have either been with a sitter, at a daycare center, at school in a late day program, or, if they're old enough, home alone.

The question on the tip of everyone's tongue? "What's for dinner?"

Chances are, there are no leftovers to reheat, simply because no one has been home to prepare a meal all week. So there's a good chance that prepared food has been picked up already at a takeout or drive-thru operation conveniently located along the route dad or mom travels from office to home. Or the evening meal may be just a phone call away, provided by an area delivery operation. The last resort is going out to eat.

Parents, who are long on guilt and short on time, will most likely let their children make the choice of where to dine. Kids under age 10 favor restaurants that take play seriously and offer immediate gratification. They appreciate being seated as soon as possible at a table served by the friendliest person on the waitstaff.

Give kids crayons and something to color. Keep them so busy that they can't cause a disturbance. Give them something to nibble on. Then, treat them to the meals that they love the best.

Recognize that they are smart, and worldly wise beyond their years. Don't patronize, but treat these tykes with respect and honor their special needs.

Remember that young children never come to a restaurant alone. Parents, who are ultimately in charge of paying, are seeking to spend quality time with the entire family. They want to eat in peace, engage in pleasant conversation, relax without fear that their offspring will be a major source of embarrassment. They, too, want selections from a preapproved food list for kids. Plus, they want smaller portions priced accordingly.

If their children are happy, well-fed, and well-behaved, parents are satisfied that they got their money's worth. They may be more inclined to return.

"For the most part, children and parents are two segmented audiences," concluded Clifford Scott. "So I think that there's a huge opportunity for marketers to attract families by taking a two-tier approach: talking to kids in a language that they understand, appealing to them as a fun, fast operation, and appealing to parents by promoting good food."

## TAKING FAMILY MATTERS TO HEART

Now the question on the tip of your tongue: Is all this extra effort worth it?

It's a matter of fact that as soon as childless households produce heirs, spending patterns change. While children and their families account for 43 percent of personal consumption expenditures for food away from home, they spend less per capita than husband-wife duos, according to the Bureau of Labor Statistics' Consumer Expenditure Survey. Kids' meals cost less and that brings down check averages.

The "up side" to catering to kids is that it gives restaurateurs another reason to attract consumers, according to outside industry observers, such as Clifford Scott.

James McNeal doesn't beat around the bush. "Restaurants have to recognize that there are only two sources of new customers, those who switch from competitors and those who are nurtured before they enter the marketplace," he said. "These are the customers who become the most loyal. Adults die. Children grow up.

"I understand why restaurants would only want adults. But if you don't want the future in your business—you don't have a future."

## HOW TO BENEFIT FROM THE BABY BOOM BONANZA

In the pages ahead, independent and multiconcept restaurateurs, quickservice and midscale chain operators, hotel food and beverage executives, airline and cruise line marketers build case after case attesting to the gains to be made by investing in families now. Many are true pioneers in this niche market, operators with kids' menus and kids' clubs dating back to the 1950s. There are also those who are just getting started, with relatively recent promotional programs and public relations campaigns aimed at catering to customers from the cradle to the grave.

The list is by no means exhaustive. Given the number of foodservice operations jumping on the baby boomlet bandwagon, it would be a formidable task to feature them all. Rather, you'll find here a representative sample of the best and the brightest, the most creative and commonsensical, the most innovative and inspiring ideas from several future-oriented operators in the industry.

## READ ON!

Now that we have had a look at the changing American family, let's shift the focus to the family restaurant. By today's expanded definition, that means any eating establishment that welcomes children.

Tables may be covered in white linen cloths, red-and-white checked vinyl, butcher block paper, or paper placemats. Seating may be at a counter, booth, poolside, or ship's captain's table. The specialty of the house may be steaks or hamburgers, pizza or pasta, ribs or chicken. Check averages for four may be $50 or $15. Whatever the ambience, mood, or food, in this world we live in, families with children are apt to show up anywhere.

Be prepared by reading on. Learn what it takes to establish a kid-friendly reputation. Discover what's new in children's menus, kids' meals, and pint-sized promotions. Learn how to form a loyal future customer base, gain exposure in the community, and forge mutually rewarding partnerships with schools. Find out how to profit from children's parties and the opportunities that result from providing special services, such as baby-sitting and valet stroller parking. The guide to suppliers of kid-related goodies will also come in handy in equipping your operation with everything from high chairs to fish nuggets in high sea shapes.

# Chapter Two

# *Setting a Kid-Friendly Scene*

Singles who came out swinging in the 1970s have since settled down, married, and begun multiplying. Many of their favorite haunts have also undergone transformations.

Take T.G.I. Friday's, for example. Twenty years ago "Let's Party" was the middle name of this Dallas, Texas, casual restaurant chain, owned by Carlson Company. Business revolved around the bar. Adults were the target market. Food took a back seat to beverages. Then, the rules of the game changed. The singles business went bust. Selling liquor lost its lure.

"We realized that we wanted to be known more as a restaurant serving beverages than as a bar serving food," said Steve Hickey, senior vice president of marketing. "In truth, we wouldn't have lasted these 27 years (and grown to 210 units) if we hadn't changed."

With its comfortable and casual atmosphere, somewhat noisy, friendly, and fun ambience, and high energy level, Friday's entered the competition for families' dining-out dollars in exceedingly great shape.

In the past decade, the operation has become even more attentive to parents and progeny. The newest restaurants are being built in suburban locations—the epicenter of the family market. They are smaller and more comfortable. Booth seating has increased. The bar is on the side, rather than center stage. And the menu features healthier foods and healthier (nonalcoholic) drinks.

Families now account for approximately 25 percent of all parties on weeknights, and up to 50 percent of business on Saturday and Sunday. The figures are even more impressive taking into consideration that children have never been the target of marketing programs or the focus of ads, according to Hickey. "But when they do come into the restaurant, we do everything we can to make sure that they have a good time."

## PLAYING THE PERFECT HOST TO THE NEXT GENERATION

Friday's has established a reputation, and built up quite an ambitious business, by creating a hospitable environment where children feel wanted and parents feel good about bringing them along. In other words, Friday's is "kid-friendly." Too new to be listed in any dictionary, the term is open to broad interpretation.

Take T.G.I. Friday's. To make children feel like very important patrons as soon as they walk through the door, the restaurant gives them helium-filled balloons imprinted with the chain's logo. The balloons are then tied to the back of their chairs, and when the kids leave, loosely tied around their wrists. They also receive individual packets of cellophane-wrapped crayons and an eight-page "Kids Only" menu filled with games, pictures to color, and descriptions of lunch/dinner and brunch items, "delicious drinks," and desserts.

Staff training is another essential ingredient in creating a kid-friendly environment. Servers are encouraged to talk directly, not down, to children. They ask kids for their orders rather than let adults be their mouthpieces. They serve kids first. They treat kids with respect.

Said Hickey, "We train our people to pay special attention to children. The ones we get are a little older, six to 12, than those frequenting fast food operations. They like the fact that this is a restaurant for grown-ups rather than a place for kids. And when they come here, they think of it as a treat.

"The thing that they most like is being treated as human beings."

## KID-FRIENDLY TIPS

Short of putting a playground in the parking lot, offering babysitting services, and hanging out a "Kids Welcome Here" sign (which, in fact, are all viable methods of wooing the family), certain signals relay immediately to customers of tableservice restaurants that kids pass muster with management.

- High chairs, sassy seats, and/or boosters are in plentiful supply.

Those who go above and beyond the call of duty for parents of infants and toddlers also provide disposable bibs, jars of baby food, and changing tables in both the ladies' and men's rooms.

- There are separate children's menus, a distinctive children's section on the regular menu, or a statement attesting to the availability of half-portions—at reduced prices—for children 12 and under.

At the very least, servers are given license to promote certain dishes that kids really like as well as sell the fact that the kitchen honors special requests for finicky little eaters.

- The waiting game is made a lot more fun.

Before being seated, children are entertained from a communal toy chest, stocked with picture books, toys, and games. The miscellaneous collection often consists of items left behind from children's previous visits. At the table, standard handouts—activity menus, placemats, or coloring sheets and crayons—keep younger children occupied until their food arrives. Note: Keep a good supply of play material in stock to avoid running out. Children are very fickle consumers and their favorite restaurant is apt to take a severe drop in the charts if their play expectations fail to be met.

- Tableware is kiddie-proof, with the emphasis on downscaling and durability.

For easy grasping, drinks are served in juice or four-ounce beverage glasses. (Note: To avoid spills, don't top off the glasses. You can always offer free refills to add value.) Plastic is preferable to glass, and bendable straws better than those that are inflexible.

Entrees come with salad forks, soup with teaspoons (and a cup of ice to speed the soup cooling process). Knives are kept as far away from kids as possible.

Tables are covered in plastic cloths. Or linen tablecloths are topped with butcher block paper.

- Staff is attentive to the needs and demands of both parents and children.

A general rule is to ask the permission of parents first on issues ranging from seating to serving. May I lift your child into the high chair? Would you like beverages brought out with entrees (to prevent children from filling up on soda pop)? Would you like children's meals served as soon as they are ready? May I bring anything else? (If parents want dessert, they'll ask for it rather than having servers suggest it.)

- Emergency measures are in place.

There are plenty of napkins on the table. If spills do occur, they are cleaned up as rapidly as possible. Items spilled are replaced, free of charge.

- Seating is in a visually stimulating area.

## KID SUPERIOR INTERIORS

Dining out is like attending the theater to children. The more excitement, drama, and action, the more memorable the experience.

When it comes to putting on a show with food, Walt Disney World Resort in Lake Buena Vista, Florida, is second to none. But the latest generation of restaurants go even further and provide "interactive dining" experiences, according to Keith Keogh, Epcot Center's executive chef.

At the Prime Time Cafe in Disney-MGM Studios Theme Park, seating is at laminate tables in 1950s-style kitchenettes. The menu matches the era, with such signature dishes as chili mac (chili over angel-hair pasta) and country-style pot roast served on Fiesta Ware dishes or three-compartment "TV dinner" trays. Video screens at each table show black-and-white clips from original sitcoms. And children, who are offered crayons and pictures to color while waiting for their food, are encouraged to hang their completed artwork on the old-fashioned refrigerator door near the 226-seat restaurant's entrance.

"I have children myself, and I find that their expectations are very high," Keogh said. "To keep them occupied, the architecture and ambience of a restaurant should be really exciting."

Meanwhile, at the Sci-Fi Dine-In Theater Restaurant, also part of Disney-MGM Studios Theme Park, guests are shown to their own 1950s-era automobiles, complete with flashy chrome, fins, and whitewalls, and painted in a rainbow of colors. The car dining booths are turned to a big screen, presenting a 45-minute special of science fiction movie trailers and cartoons. Kids watch while they dine on any one of six entrees featured on their own menu, including "Space Strips" of chicken served with curly fries or a fruit cup and the "Junior Red Planet," assorted fresh seasonal vegetables in a tomato herb sauce over linguine.

"The only way restaurateurs are going to survive is to give customers something more than they can get at home," Keogh predicted.

Without going to the extent and expense of Disney, here are some ways to add more energy to the dining environment and attract more kid biz.

- Book clowns or jugglers to entertain children at Saturday lunch or Sunday brunch.
- Offer cooking demonstrations periodically to break up monotony. Consider investing in a "Mickey Mouse Waffle Maker." Or show kids how to flip pizza dough. Keep the lessons short and simple.
- If space allows, set up an electric train or an aquarium.
- If space allows, create a separate game room.
- If nothing else, seat children by a window so they can watch the parade of pedestrians and vehicles passing by.

## SNACK SAMPLER

Giving children something to munch on—to ease hunger and ward off boredom while waiting—is a relatively inexpensive way to gain additional favor with families. Take inventory of the items that you already have in stock or feature on the salad bar, and single out those with the widest kid appeal. Some ideas include:

- Breadsticks
- Single servings of oyster and soda crackers
- Cheese cubes
- Mini-cups of soup
- Applesauce
- Carrot and celery sticks, cucumber slices, cherry tomatoes, red and green pepper rings, broccoli florets
- Orange slices (from the bar), apple and melon chunks, grape clusters, whole strawberries, whatever is in season and available

- Popcorn
- Plain, cooked rice or pasta in easy-to-pick-up shapes
- Cheerios (for the very young)

After the meal, ask parents first if it is all right to reward members of the clean plate club. Then serve any of the following:

- Cookies in fun shapes, such as teddy bear or dinosaur grahams or fortune cookies (you don't have to be a Chinese restaurant to offer them)
- Penny lollipops
- Frozen novelties, such as ice pops
- A mini-scoop or mini-cone of ice cream or frozen yogurt
- Whole fruit, such as "shiny red" apples or oranges
- Gold foil-wrapped mints

## LAST RESORTS

Even the most well-behaved little angels experience occasional bad days. If you find that children's lapses in conduct are disrupting the dining room, here are some intervention tactics.

- Avoid unnecessary disasters with very young and very active children by clearing the table of salt and pepper shakers, sugar dispensers, candles, extra placesettings, extra glassware, and the like.
- The next best thing to crayons and coloring sheets are pens and paper bags, which can be transformed into puppets.
- Children may enjoy pretending to be part of the waitstaff. Supply them with a pen and server's pad, and see if that doesn't settle them down.
- A visit to the kitchen is another ploy to help restless kids pass the time in peace. A staff member who has some down time

can conduct the tour. Keep a Polaroid camera on hand, and offer to take the children's pictures with the chef.

- If kids are old enough, set them up at a station with a simple task to perform (rolling out pizza dough, peeling potatoes, spooning out salad dressing, calling out orders).

- If all else fails, bring out the check and disposable containers, and offer to pack up the meal for the family to consume at home.

## OPERATORS SPEAK OUT

Some have taken elaborate measures to insure a place in the family market. Others have simply modified standard operating procedures. Obviously, there are a myriad of ways to roll out the red carpet to parents and children as you are about to discover while reading through the case studies of kid-friendly operators featured in this book.

## ADVENTURES IN BABY-SITTING

Parents of young children may elect to dine out with their brood in tow or run up a tab at home by leaving a baby-sitter in charge of the charges. A third option, now available at select restaurants around the country, is to take out the kids and then turn them over to an in-house care giver for the duration of the meal.

All three Rockwells American Restaurants in Westchester County, New York, chose the latter option, to satisfy the needs of the family-oriented operation's target market. Parents get a break, and kids are assured of a great time, according to restaurant spokesperson Barbara Gentile.

"We felt that offering this option to our customers enhanced our image that we are not only a friendly, casual, all-American restaurant, but also one with truly something for everyone—including the parents who deliberate between staying home and dragging children out for a less-than-relaxing dining experience," said Gentile. "As a foodservice establishment, this also helps increase the traffic on particularly slow evenings."

On Monday, Tuesday, and Wednesday nights, and occasional weekday afternoons, designated space in the main or private dining rooms of each restaurant is cordoned off and transformed into a large-scale play area with educational toys, books, coloring books, and crayons for kids to enjoy alone or in the company of new-found friends. Hostesses are relieved of their posts on these traditionally slow traffic turn-outs to serve as sitters—a welcome reassignment. Gentile said, "They look forward to the opportunity to do it. Some of them are especially creative with the kids."

The service is entirely free though there is a charge for food; selections come from the children's menu, such as English muffin pizzas, baby burgers with fries, and ziti with tomato sauce, and are priced from $2.95 to $3.95. And to keep tables turning, there is a time limit, set at 75 minutes.

Rockwells advertises the child care offer on tabletents (see Figure 2–1), in local newspapers, and via radio on commercial spots. But word-of-mouth has been an exceptional medium in getting the message across to the community, according to Gentile.

At A Piece of Quiet in Denver, Colorado, owners Sally Rock and husband Dale Goin have gone one step farther. They've created an entirely separate, adult-supervised restaurant for their patrons' children. The Kids Cafe, located adjacent to the 35-seat formal dining room, is visible through a one-way mirrored wall dividing the two operations. So children, literally, can be seen, but not heard.

"My husband and I were both single parents when we met, and we were acutely aware of how difficult it can be to take children out to eat at a fine restaurant," said Rock. "Segregation seemed to be the perfect solution."

Guests phone in reservations, giving the day, time, number in their party, and the ages and sexes of their children. This latter information is necessary in preparing the playroom and maintaining a five to one ratio of children to care givers, according to Rock. At this point, children are instructed to phone another number for a recorded message explaining The Kids Cafe dining experience.

# ADVENTURES IN BABYSITTING!

Relax...enjoy your dinner! Every Monday,
Tuesday and Wednesday night, Rockwells
offers you our special babysitting service
from 5pm - 9pm complete with
## ACTIVITY CENTER
## STORYTIME
## ARTS & CRAFTS
And don't forget to ask our manager about
Lunch Time Babysitting Services, too!!
(Space Limited • Child's Time Limited to 1 hr. 15 minutes)

Figure 2-1    Tabletent child care offer (courtesy of Rockwells
American Restaurants, Westchester, NY)

Upon arrival at A Piece of Quiet, adults enter through one door
while children open another into The Cafe and walk into a world
where everything is scaled down to their size. The space owes much
of its energy and interest to multilevels with vibrant color coming

from the brightly painted wall murals of an Italian street scene, created by a set designer from the Denver Center for the Performing Arts. There are tables and chairs for feasting on fun food or just plain having fun with the toys, books, art projects, and videos stocked on the shelves.

"We try to get the children seated and eating as soon as we can," said Rock. They are greeted with "Antipasta" (before the pasta) or snacks of apples, carrots, juice, and milk. Then, they select their main course. Items range from "Itty-Bitty Ziti" (kid-sized tube pasta with cheese sauce) to "Silly Fusilli" (red, green, and white curly pasta with butter) to "Dirt for Dessert." This signature dish consists of creamy chocolate pudding served in a flower pot, and topped with finely crushed Oreo cookies, a gummy worm, and a plastic flower. The fixed price of $5 also includes two hours of supervised play.

Rock designed the menu (see Figure 2–2) as well as many of the games and activities that occupy children's time before and after dinner. One magnetic game board, complete with forks, spoons, and knives, instructs children on how to set the table properly. Another enables them to personalize a pizza, with magnetic tomatoes, pepperoni, even anchovies. A game designed around restaurant manners teaches players to say phrases such as "My compliments to the chef," "Service was excellent," and "May I have the check," and how to calculate tips. For restaurant role playing, there are chef and waiter uniforms to dress up in. Another activity features four-color photos of food, originally found in magazines, which are cut in half and pasted on white paper. Children get to complete the picture.

For her ingenious "little" restaurant, Rock has amassed tremendous local, national, and international publicity and can list among her patrons visitors coming from as far away as Tokyo, Japan. Yet business has not been all a bed of roses. Said Rock, "Since this is like no other restaurant, ever, we do have to respond to a whole set of new problems. The kids arrive at different times. They are all different ages. Their parents suffer separation anxiety. If children cry, the parents won't stay. Other times, children cry and won't leave the restaurant.

# MENU
FIXED PRICE: $5⁰⁰
(INCLUDES 2 HOURS
SUPERVISED PLAY)

**ANTIPASTA** (BEFORE THE PASTA) - SALAD WITH COLD MEATS, CHEESES, FRUITS, VEGETABLES & CRACKERS

**ITTY-BITTY ZITI** - KID-SIZED TUBE PASTA WITH CHEESE SAUCE

**SILLY FUSILLI** - RED, GREEN & WHITE CURLY PASTA WITH BUTTER

**SPAGHETTI** - "LITTLE STRINGS" PASTA WITH TOMATO SAUCE

**PIZZA** - CHEESE OR PEPPERONI

**BEVERAGES** - MILK, CHOCOLATE MILK, STRAWBERRY MILK, JUICE, OR LEMONADE

**DIRT FOR DESSERT** - CHOCOLATE PUDDING WITH CRUMBLED OREOS & A GUMMY WORM SERVED IN A FLOWER POT

OR **DINOSAUR COOKIES**

ALSO:

**STARTERS FOR THE "JUST STARTING"** BABY FOOD, ZWIEBACK TOAST, & RICE CAKES

Figure 2-2   Children's menu (courtesy of A Piece of Quiet, Denver, CO)

"It's difficult to turn tables because most parents of young children prefer dining early. It's also difficult to get people to frequent the restaurant during the week."

Developing special coupon promotions with the local Gymboree, an indoor playground franchise organization, has proven to be a successful method of stirring up more traffic. Rewarding repeat customers with money-off incentives has also helped increase frequency.

The one obstacle Rock never faced was getting insurance. She said, "In this state, with our particular agent, the feeling was that it's safer to corral kids in their own child-proof space than to have them run free around waiters delivering hot food."

After listening to enough guests say that they'd come to his restaurant more often if only they could get a baby-sitter, Steve Bryne of the 124-seat Bistro Banlieue in Lombard, Illinois, investigated opening an on-premises childcare center. But plans were soon scrapped when he began adding up costs. "They were astronomical," he said.

In seeking a more cost-effective alternative, Bryne worked out an arrangement with KinderCare. The facility, one of many childcare centers located within the vicinity of his suburban Chicago operation, happened to be the only one licensed to be open at night. Bistro Banlieue pays the fee for the visit of up to two children per family. KinderCare is responsible for everything else.

"The service is just something we offer," said Bryne. "Initially, we received a lot of coverage from the press. But we don't promote it a lot. We probably get guests using it once every two weeks."

## SATURDAY IS FAMILY DAY

To eat really well in Chicago on a Saturday, the general rule is to wait for dinner. That's when most of the finer restaurants finally open for business.

But waiving lunch in anticipation of the late date night crowd has never been part of the program at Frontera Grill, one of the country's most celebrated authentic Mexican restaurants and top of the list of most popular dining haunts in the Windy City. "We opened for Saturday lunch at the same time we opened for business in March of 1987," said chef-proprietor Rick Bayless, who with wife Deann also oversees the adjoining, and more upscale, 48-seat Topolobampo. "We verbally encouraged people we knew who had kids to come down in the morning, beginning at 10:30 A.M. It's really laid-back. The atmosphere is more relaxed. We can give more personal attention than in the evening hours when the place gets jammed."

Word spread, and now Saturday is Frontera Grill's busiest lunch of the week. Appealing to families is also proving to be a worthwhile long-term investment. "We are sealing bonds with customers," said Bayless.

There is plenty for children to love off the regular menu, including quesadillas, which Bayless refers to as Mexico's answer to toasted cheese sandwiches. But the main attraction is in the back-of-the-house, where children are taken for informal tortilla-making lessons. Servers, many of whom are parents themselves, volunteer to accompany the children to the kitchen, where they can watch and learn how to prepare this Mexican staple.

## STROLLER VALET PARKING PROGRAM

Traffic jams are common at South Coast Plaza Mall in Costa Mesa, California, caused by the steady stream of strollers being pushed around by shoppers. The Back Bay Rowing & Running Club's solution to clear the congestion that often builds at the restaurant's entrance is stroller valet parking service.

Moms, dads, or sitters roll children into the casual eatery. Then, the strollers are tagged with claim checks bearing the restaurant's name and a number, and are parked in designated spaces alongside the 34-foot salad bar. Attendants (alias members of the staff) retrieve the moving vehicles after the meal. As customers stroll back into the mall, the claim check tag that is still attached acts as a walking advertisement for the restaurant.

There is no charge for the service, a fact promoted on an 8″ ×

10″ sign posted beneath the cash register. The notice also acts to increase customers' comfort levels by informing them that kids are welcome, according to Don Bruyn, general manager.

"Stroller parking is just one part of our ongoing program to make our restaurant kid-friendly," said Hal Rosoff, Back Bay's president.

Bruyn added, "Our philosophy is you don't have to go out of your way and give kids expensive boxed meals. If you want to take care of the family, get down on your knees and talk to children at eye level.

"As far as entertainment goes, we buy a big box of Crayola crayons and put a few in a glass at a time for each child. We also buy a few coloring books to use in the restaurant. Or we'll give them the small Number 12 white bags, which we use for take out, to color and make into puppets.

"These kids are my future customers. We want this to be their destination restaurant."

Stroller valet parking is also part of an ongoing program to serve families with young children at Paul's Place, an upscale fast food chain with three locations in the Denver area. Strollers are parked in their own outside lot and tagged. Rather than numbers, the tickets are illustrated with pictures ranging from Santa to a star. To retrieve their four-wheelers, children simply turn in their claim checks.

"Families are a big part of our business," said Al Marcove, owner. "Kids really feel comfortable when they come here."

It's understandable, given the special treatment that they receive. Open the menu, and the statement "We Love Kids" is actually spelled out. (See Figure 2–3.) At their seats, the objects of Paul's affection receive placemats, which they are free to play with and purchase. The water-filled mats, custom-made for the restaurant, feature a "find the food" game.

Children's meals, consisting of a choice of char-burgers, hot dogs, or "Chicken Dippers," come with fries, a small drink, and a trip to the self-serve ice cream and frozen fruit dessert sundae bar stocked with 10 different toppings.

Before leaving, children receive a balloon and a toy, which they pick from a big toy basket brought to the table by a hostess. The

## FRIES & ONION RINGS

| | Regular | Medium | Basket |
|---|---|---|---|
| **FRENCH FRIES** Made fresh daily. | .89 | 1.39 | 2.49 |
| **CURLY FRIES** Seasoned | 1.09 | 1.59 | 2.69 |
| **CHEDDAR FRIES** With nacho cheese. | 1.29 | 1.79 | 3.09 |
| **ONION RINGS** Thinly sliced and uniquely spiced | .99 | 1.59 | 2.89 |

## HM✔ HEALTHMARK ITEMS

**CHAR • BURGER** 95% Lean     3.99
Served with lettuce and tomato on a multi-grain bun.

**LITE CHICKEN**     3.99
Char-broiled chicken breast marinated in terriyaki.

**SMOKED TUNA STEAK**     4.49
Char-broiled tuna served on a multi-grain bun with lettuce, tomato, and our special sauce.

**VEGETARIAN CHILI** Meatless     1.89

## SIDE DISHES

| | |
|---|---|
| **SALAD BAR** (All you can eat) | 3.49 |
| **SALAD BAR** (One Trip) | 1.79 |
| **SALAD BAR** (One Trip) With any Sandwich | 1.39 |
| **CHILI** Paul's Original | 2.09 |
| **SOUP OF THE DAY** Home cooked | 2.29 |

## PAUL'S Signature ITEMS

## DESSERTS

**OLD-FASHIONED MILKSHAKES**     2.49
Made with hard ice cream and topped with fresh whipped cream. Chocolate, Vanilla, Strawberry or Jamoca, plus a flavor of the month

**ICE CREAM FLOATS**     1.99

**CHOCOLATE WAFFLE**     3.19
1/4 Waffle with any items from our frozen dessert bar

**FROZEN DESSERT BAR**     2.89
Ice cream and a 100% natural fruit treat.

## BELGIAN WAFFLE BAR (6:30 a.m. to 10:30 a.m.)

Try our Belgian Waffle Bar with as many as 15 unique toppings such as Vermont maple syrup, strawberry champagne sauce, bananas Grand Marnier and peach melba, as well as fresh fruit. We also have many Healthmark approved toppings

| | |
|---|---|
| **THE WAFFLE BAR** | 4.29 |
| HM✔ **HEALTHMARK WAFFLE** | 4.29 |
| **APPLE SMOKED BACON** | 2.29 |
| **CHICKEN & APPLE SAUSAGE** | 2.49 |

## WE LOVE Kids

## DRINKS

**BOTTOMLESS SOFT DRINKS, LEMONADE OR ICED TEA**     .99

**VERNORS'**     .99

**FRESH SQUEEZED ORANGE JUICE** 1.79
Breakfast hours only.

**SHARPS NON-ALCOHOLIC BEER**     1.79

**COFFEE, HOT TEA, OR MILK**     .79

## KIDS MENU

**KID'S PURE BEEF HOT DOG** 2.39 • **KID'S CHAR•BURGER** 2.39 • **KID'S CHICKEN DIPPERS** 2.99
All Kid's Meals include fries, small drink and a trip to the frozen dessert bar.

Figure 2-3 "We Love Kids" menu (courtesy of Paul's Place, Denver, CO)

selection is a mixed bag—everything from spinning tops to baseball cards and finger monsters. And it changes frequently as an incentive to return.

"Children don't like to get the same toys. We change them every three to four days so they'll want to come back," said Marcove.

## KIDS GET STAR TREATMENT

The American Cafe's open door policy toward kids is a relatively recent phenomenon, which resulted when it became obvious that the midscale restaurant chain's core customer base of young urban professionals was starting to settle down to rear families.

"Our clientele changed considerably over a 15-year period. All of a sudden, yuppies were becoming young parents," said Julia Obici, director of marketing. At all 18 restaurants, dispersed along the Washington, D.C. Beltway to Baltimore, Maryland, and beyond, "We wanted to make sure that parents with small children felt welcome, which meant training our waitstaff specifically to accommodate their needs."

How to treat "rising stars" (a term used by The American Cafe to refer to its youngest customers) now takes up a special section in the chain's employee training manual. Here is the list of servers' tips, designed to make every family's visit to the restaurant a pleasure:

- At your first approach, be sure that high chairs and boosters have been properly taken care of.
- Be sure the children are out of the aisles.
- Make sure they've received their children's placemat, crayons, and a balloon.
- Get a small plate with three Melba toast and three carrot sticks as quickly as possible.
- Serve beverages in short glasses with a straw. A cherry is a nice treat.

- Offer to bring out their food right away.
- Never refill soft drinks or bring food out when not requested to do so. Always ask.
- A damp napkin or a few extra "bevnaps" are helpful when left on the table. "Floor awareness" is especially important.
- Baby food and bottles can be warmed in the kitchen, but have the parents check the temperature themselves.
- Never serve children their food on hot plates.

Training appears to be paying off handsomely. According to Obici, "Response has been excellent. We get letters commending our servers."

Parents also appreciate the fact that all kids' meals are priced at $1.95. Favorite selections include spaghetti (called "Pa-Sket-te" on the menu) and meatballs, chicken tenders, and cheese pizza. For dessert, the top choice is "The Messiest Sundae," featuring vanilla ice cream, hot fudge, crumbled cookies, and whipped cream.

## SECRET HIDING PLACE ENCHANTS CHILDREN

The Angus Barn in Raleigh, North Carolina, is a high-volume, high-check average, high-quality steak house—not your typical family restaurant. And yet, in the last few years, parents accompanied by their children have been patronizing the 600-seat white tablecloth restaurant with increasing frequency.

"People who are reluctant to hire baby-sitters are bringing their children to dine with us," said Van Eure, co-owner with mother Alice Eure of the 32-year-old fine dining institution. "We really haven't met a child so far that we haven't been able to please."

Eure added, "We keep them so entertained that they don't have time to create disturbances."

The experience begins the moment a child walks through the Barn's front door and is greeted in the lobby with two thick volumes containing letters of appreciation from previous young guests. "We save every letter we receive from children and post them in two huge books," said Eure. The record of correspondences serves to assure new customers that children are welcome. Returning customers are delighted to find their letters featured.

Upon being seated, each child is then handed a balloon, along with an Angus Barn coloring book and crayons. Recognizing that it is a challenge for kids to sit for one-and-a-half to two hours while parents enjoy a leisurely, relaxing dinner, children are also given a water-filled placemat containing a game. "If they still look fidgety, either a waitress, hospitality hostess, or bus boy will take them on a tour of the kitchen," said Eure. "Many of the older children are so fascinated with being behind-the-scenes, we'll give them uniforms and put them to work, performing small tasks such as turning steaks."

Each child also gets a small gift from Eure's "secret hiding place." Little toy trinkets and treasures are stowed away in a cubby hole upstairs in the Barn's loft area. "Because it's a secret that only kids know about, they get so excited," said Eure. "If you can make children happy, look what you've done for the parents.

"This is a situation where good things have come from good things. Now when parents ask their children where they want to go to eat, they say Angus Barn."

## COWBOY BUB'S BUCKAROOS PASS THE TIME AWAY IN PLAYFUL PURSUIT OF BUB BUCKS

With Bub City Crabshack & Bar-B-Q, specializing in Southern comfort food served funky, down-home style, Lettuce Entertain You Enterprises, Inc. has made a valuable contribution to Chicago's diversified dining scene. The informal restaurant, which seats 550 at tables covered in red-and-white checked plastic cloths, newsprint, and butcher block paper, has been purposely designed to look distressed, weathered, worn, aged beyond its three years. With country music blaring over the loudspeakers and high, paneled ceilings muffling the sounds of babies crying and toddlers whining, it's just the kind of casual and fun environment parents feel confident walking into with children.

"We've always attracted a lot of families," said Bob Vick, vice president of Lettuce. So a kids' menu and kids' club, called Cowboy Bub's Buckaroos, were created. But after discussions with his in-house staff and partners, many of whom are parents, Vick decided to do something more for this facet of the market, and convert a private dining room into a game room during regular operating hours every Sunday.

The room is advantageously positioned in the back of the restaurant. "Parents feel comfortable because children are close enough to be seen, but they are also out of sound range," said Vick. To build a sense of security, there are two staffers, who are employed as teachers during the work week, overseeing the games and leading group activities.

"We started small, with very simplistic games appealing to kids 10 and under. They're the ones traditionally getting impatient while waiting at tables," said Vick. "We consulted with quite a few of our waitresses, who are teachers, to find out what would work with this age group."

Then, Bub City entered into an agreement with a local entertainment company to produce and maintain the games. The attractions include a frisbee toss, in which players aim for the hole in the chest of a wooden cowboy; a ring toss, in which the objective is to land plastic rings around the neck of Coca-Cola bottles arranged in a display; a coin toss, in which kids attempt to land imitation gold coins on saucers floating around a pool; and a dart game, in which players shoot rubber-suctioned darts at Bub City logos imprinted on a target board. Spin art (creating pictures by splattering paint) and a bean bag toss through a swinging tire are the two newest activities to entice first-time guests and the growing number of repeat customers.

All those who play win Bub Bucks, little wooden coins that may be redeemed for real toys off a prize board. "We're also talking about doing something with a charge card that would be tied into our gift store," said Vick. Players who earn a certain number of points would be able to move up to a higher level of quality merchandise, stocked on the shelves. "This gives the kids a shopping expedition and an incentive to return (to score more points toward a prize)," Vick added.

During the week, the private party room converts back to its original function—as a stage for private parties. Games are stored on the ceiling, rigged up by a series of ropes. Given the eclectic look of the restaurant, they seem to fit right in with the decor, according to Vick. He said, "Come Sunday, it takes three hours from start to finish to set up the room." Games come down. Barrels and haystacks are set out to make the space more intimate. Sing-along children's tapes are piped into the room.

The extra energy exerted in creating such a playful environment seems to be paying off. Vick said, "Our Sunday business has almost doubled, and it's only getting better."

## "KIDSTALL" STACKED WITH KIDS' FAVORITE FOODS

Zoopa, Restaurants Unlimited, Inc.'s soup-salad-pasta-fruit-muffin-dessert bar concept was originally intended to meet specific needs of grazers and health-conscious consumers. It was developed for adults who had grown up on fast food and were now seeking more sophisticated dining options, fresher presentations, the convenience of self-service, and a flexible pricing structure. But a funny thing happened when the Seattle-area multifood station operation opened in 1990: Families with children adopted the concept.

"Zoopa is a smash with kids, not entirely by design," confessed spokesperson Rick Perkal. "They like it for the same reasons that adults do. It's casual. There are a lot of foods that they like. And they are free to choose what they want to eat. Our price points (average check of $6.50 for adults; children 12 and under, half-price; those under 5 eat free) also allow parents to bring in kids.

"So it made sense to give families even more reason to feel welcome."

The kid-friendly ambience kicks off at the front door, where high chairs with wheels for easy strolling are positioned. Then, next

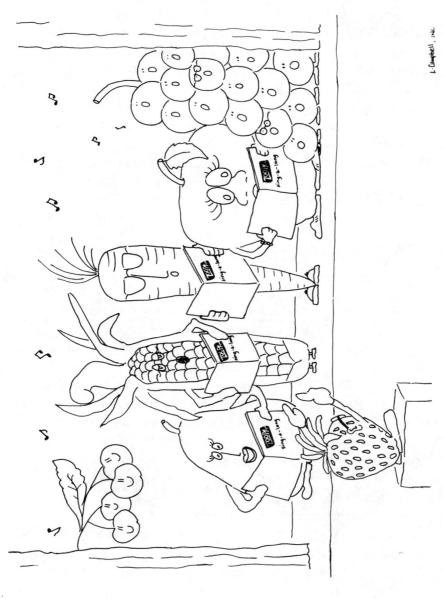

Figure 2-4 Coloring sheet with singing vegetables (courtesy of Zoopa, Restaurants Unlimited, Inc., Seattle, WA)

to the trays and napkin-wrapped silverware, and under the brightly lettered sign, "Zoopakids," are three bins: one containing kids' bibs, another holding coloring sheets, and a third filled with paper cups packed with crayons.

There are three different coloring sheets, printed specifically for the 205-seat restaurant. In keeping with Zoopa's accent on freshness, one features a chorus of singing vegetables. (See Figure 2–4.) Another features a dot-to-dot that spells out "We (heart) Zoopas."

"Children are free to select from the elaborate offerings that we're already extending to guests," said Perkal. Or they may pass up the two 60-foot long salad bars, stacked with fresh salad fixings, the specialty salad bar with 15 to 20 different prepared items, the two pasta dishes, five varieties of soup, an extensive array of fresh fruits, baked-on-premises muffins, breads, and desserts offered daily at respective stations. And they may make a beeline to the "Kidstall" kiosk, featuring such favorites as Cheerios, pretzels, breadsticks, GoldFish crackers, yogurt-covered raisins, and carrot sticks and broccoli.

All of the items are finger foods, according to Perkal. They are also easy to see and within easy reach because the bar stands just three feet high.

One other feature makes Zoopa a popular parents' choice. There are changing tables in both the ladies' and men's rooms.

## NEIGHBORHOOD FAVORITES

The kiddie ride parked at the entrance of Two Boots, and the sign that reads "Kids Welcome" painted in bright red letters on the glass facade, leave absolutely no doubt with passersby that the 60-seat restaurant and pizzeria on Manhattan's Lower East Side is a friend to families.

Living up to its claim, the atmosphere inside is comfortable, casual, and very homey. There's a small, six-seat bar area, with spinning stools that kids find irresistible. Another draw is the open kitchen, where the show of pizzas being prepared consistently wins raves from young audiences.

If that's not enough to keep kids occupied, picture books and toys left behind by previous diners, coloring books, and crayons delivered in plastic, animal-shaped cups are given out automatically, according to manager Janet Henry.

"We cater to parents with kids," she said. "This is a real neighborhood place. Compared to the rest of Manhattan, the area is affordable to young families. Those who live around here come in for lunch or early in the evening for dinner. Then they leave, and the crowd turns older."

The adult menu, offering Cajun and Italian specialties, also features a kids' section, listing waffles with fruit, scrambled eggs with a muffin, and French toast sticks ($3.95 each) for brunch; spaghetti ($2.95), ravioli ($3.95), and catfish sticks ($3.95) for dinner. (The owner's son is credited with the illustration.) Another popular option is "Pizza Face" ($4.95), a four-slice, thin crust pie topped with mild sauce, cheese, and vegetables to create the eyes, nose, mouth, and ears.

"Sometimes the pizza men go crazy and give it spiked hair," said Henry.

The restaurant rarely stages promotions without extending invitations to all the regulars, kids included. To celebrate its fifth anniversary, for instance, each child received a cookie cut into the number five, and got to help color in the big fives that were hung from the walls.

Meanwhile, across the country in Aspen, Colorado, the original Boogie's Diner has also achieved success by satisfying the parents-with-young-children niche. "Before Boogie's, there wasn't a place in town to bring kids," said general manager Bernie Mysior. "This is a cool hangout."

The unique retail outlet-restaurant, with the motto "Eat Heavy, Dress Cool," serves diner favorites while rock-and-roll music blasts over loudspeakers and covers any disturbing sounds that children might make.

Kids are treated to crayons and placemats to color (featuring an image created by Mysior's daughter) and entertained by the wait-staff, who have been known to stick straws in their ears to solicit smiles. The servers also operate under pseudonyms, such as Bif or

Your Royal Bifness, Rock, and Spike, keeping in character with the 1950s fun theme.

The concept appears to be working since there are now Boogie's Diners in Los Angeles, California; New York, New York; Washington, D.C.; Memphis, Tennessee; Las Vegas, Nevada; and Chicago, Illinois.

## CHILDREN'S CURIOSITY CORNER

Families in the market for a satisfying dining experience get more than they bargained for at Happy Joe's Superstore, a mega-eating and entertainment complex in Davenport, Iowa, housing a pizza and ice cream parlor, a bakery and banquet facility, plus a museum for mini-customers. The Children's Curiosity Corner, located on the lower level of the 12,000-square-foot facility, features 35 hands-on exhibits donated by area businesses.

Courtesy of the western wear shop is a life-size replica of a horse, riding gear, and cowboy clothing to enable youngsters to dress up, saddle up, mount up, and ride into the (pretend) sunset. Thanks to Channel 8, a news anchor desk provides future broadcast journalists with a platform to practice presentation skills. Due to the generosity of the Quad City Thunder, the region's professional basketball team, kids get to dunk baskets in a ball cage wearing players' uniforms and size 15 shoes. The fence company's contribution, a white picket fence, encloses a toddler play area equipped with age-specific educational toys.

"Probably our number one attraction is a miniature replica of a real grocery store," said Bob Schneden, director of public relations. "Children push small carts up and down the aisle, then take their pretend purchases to the checkout counter, where groceries are scanned and sales rung up on the cash register."

They also have the opportunity to play radio announcers and spin discs at a mock radio station, fulfill fantasies to become firemen, transform into librarians and check out books with a computer, even make an offer on a dream home while house-hunting in a subdivision.

Customer demands were originally what motivated Davenport-based Happy Joe's, a chain of 78 pizza and ice cream parlors located throughout the Midwest, to branch into the super store concept. Said Schneden, "We've always been family-oriented. But as competition for family dollars increased in recent years, we wanted to make sure we'd continue attracting this market.

"Parents told us that they loved our place, but were tired of giving their children quarters to plug into video games. The novelty of pizza birthday parties was also wearing thin. So we took these comments and came up with the Children's Curiosity Corner."

According to Schneden, business and industry sponsors readily lined up to participate in the program, lured by the offer of free positive publicity. "They love the arrangement because of the exposure they receive," he said.

"So far, our business has been unbelievable," added Schneden, who estimated entertaining some 100,000 visitors in the first year of operation and often staging up to 30 birthday parties a day.

Exhibitors are responsible for setting up and maintaining their displays. "If something breaks down, they fix it," said Schneden. With a full-time coordinator, plus a handful of part-time employees overseeing museum operations, Happy Joe's is left to do what it knows best: preparing and serving food.

Schneden also stresses that Children's Curiosity Corner is not a baby-sitting service. "The last thing we want is for parents to drop off their kids and leave," he said. Rather, children are under constant surveillance on television monitors, strategically placed throughout the upper level dining room.


## ALL ABOARD!

Casey's Caboose in Killington, Vermont, was built around two turn-of-the-century railroad cars—as the name implies, a caboose and a 35-ton plow car.

To say the least, the family restaurant offers "neat seating" that kids find hard to resist, according to spokesperson Casey Crompton. The most coveted spots are on the observation deck of the plow car and in the caboose's bunk area, reached by climbing up a five-foot ladder.

Railroad memorabilia adorns the walls. A live lobster tank welcomes patrons walking into the bar area. And behind the bar, an "intriguing" male skier figure hangs from a wire. Push a button on the toy, and a model train makes a loop around the restaurant's ceiling.

The train doesn't run on a regular schedule. "A local habit of frequent customers is to throw quarters at the little guy to try to trigger the train," said Crompton. Otherwise, every time the bartender receives a good tip, he'll hit the switch. A child entering the restaurant is another reason to "let 'er rip."

"When we hear a child crying, we also hit the button and let the train go around," said Crompton. Casey's Caboose has very few teary-eyed customers.

The 90-seat restaurant's kids' menu is another source of delight. (See Figure 2–5.) It is long in both listings and actual length, with the line-up spanning four different kinds of chicken dishes, three seafood entrees, and two pastas, in addition to burgers, dogs, steak, prime rib, barbecued ribs, and pork chops. The selection is taken right from the adult menu, but portions are smaller and prices are reduced accordingly.

## SPANGLES IS ON THE FAMILY TRACK

Now that so many women are working outside the home, families are turning to restaurants to satisfy cravings for hearty, home-cooked meals. Old-fashioned, all-American, moderately priced food, such as "Three-Cheese Macaroni" and "Mom's Meatloaf," is certainly one reason for the success of Spangles. Unique decor that is a catchy attention-grabber with kids is another.

The focal point of this popular parent and child hangout in Brentwood, California, is a scale model train that travels around the perimeter of the cozy dining room on a 120-foot track suspended from the ceiling. An engine pulling six cargo cars, loaded with stuffed animals and assorted toys that are always changing, traverses

# CASEY'S CABOOSE

# KID'S MENU

Smaller Portions — Smaller Prices

### "SOMETHING FOR <u>ALL</u> SIZES"
The following come with french fries with the exception of pasta dishes
"12 and Under"

## BURGERS & DOGS

**HAMBURGER** 4 oz. . . . 3.95

**CHEESEBURGER** 4 oz. . . . 4.25

**BACON CHEESE-
  BURGER** 4 oz. . . . 4.50

**HOT DOG**. . . .3.95

**BAGEL DOG -**
Cheddarwurst Dog Wrapped in Bagel Dough . . . .

# BEEF & PORK

**N.Y. SIRLOIN**
7 oz. Steak charbroiled . . . 9.95

**PRIME RIB**
8oz. cut topped with au jus . . .9.95

**B.B.Q. RIBS**
Pork rib smothered in B.B.Q. sauce . . . 6.95

**PORK CHOPS**
8 oz. center cut charbroiled . . . 7.95

# CHICKEN

**DEEP FRIED CHICKEN**
3 Pieces of honey dipped chicken . . . 6.95

**CHICKEN TERIYAKI**
6 oz. boneless breast charbroiled . . . 7.95

**CHICKEN PARMESAN**
4 oz. Breast smothered in Marinara sauce &
melted cheese . . . 5.95

**BONELESS CHICKEN TENDERS**
Breaded & Deep fried . . . 6.95

# SEAFOOD

**BROILED SCALLOPS**
Generous portion lightly breaded and broiled . . . 7.95

**SHRIMP SCAMPI**
3 butterflied sauteed shrimp . . . 8.95

**KING CRAB LEGS**
8 oz. steamed legs & claws . . . market price

# PASTA

**LINGUINE**
Topped with a zesty marinara sauce . . . 4.95

**MANICOTTI**
Two Cheese-stuffed manicotti smothered in marinara
sauce topped with melted provolone . . . 6.95

Figure 2-5   Kids' menu (courtesy of Casey's Caboose, Killington, VT)

bridges, whizzes by the pastoral landscape setting painted on one wall, and crosses the country as it passes over the U.S. map painted on another.

The train runs 14 hours a day, seven days a week, whistling whenever another order is ready to be picked up and served. Children who can't sit still or have behaved exceptionally well are often bestowed with the top honor—pushing the button that makes the whistle blow.

Kids of all ages love the attraction, according to Michael Heintz, general manager, who estimates that the family trade accounts for 50 percent of Spangles' business. "We're in a unique niche by being the only restaurant in the immediate area catering to kids," he said. As a bonus, "We often get parents coming back independently without their children to dine with us."

A portion of the adult menu is posted as the "Kids' Corner" and lists six different items, including the restaurant's signature macaroni and cheese ($4.25). The dish is served with a steamed vegetable medley of broccoli, carrots, zucchini, and cauliflower. Another popular offering is the one-quarter-pound turkey burger ($4.25). "Kids think that it's beef," said Heintz.

No homey, stick-to-the-ribs meal is complete without a gooey, rich dessert. Spangles satisfies with "Mocha Heath Bar Crunch" and "Snicker Bar" cakes. Oreo cookies served with a glass of milk for drinking and dunking are another top offering that both adults and kids find irresistible.

## LOOK UP AT THE CEILING! IS IT A BIRD? IS IT A PLANE?

Is it a train? Well, not exactly. At Fritz's Restaurant in Kansas City, Kansas, a unique mode of transportation is employed to deliver food. Burgers, chicken sandwiches, fishwiches, and other assorted hand-held compositions are packaged in boxes, then expressed to customers via a 12-volt, heater meter-generated contraption that runs on overhead tracks. At each destination point, the boxes are lowered via a mini-platform elevator, which is pumped up and down by a hydraulic jack. Customers remove their food; the box is raised and then continues on its journey back to the kitchen. Total round-trip traveling time is approximately 90 seconds.

"People call it a train, but it's not really. It's like a little shuttle that operates sort of on the same principle as slot cars," said owner Fred Kropf, whose father invented the system out of parts of motors and different wheels in the 1970s.

There is no doubt, however, that the what-d'ya-call-it has become a real draw, luring families from miles away. And as long as customers perceive that it's a train, Kropf is pleased to perpetuate the theme. On the walls of the 75-seat restaurant hang old railroad photos, and each child gets a paper engineer's cap as soon as he or she is seated. Bells sound, horns blast, and train whistles go off whenever orders are sent out.

Another novel, kid-pleasing touch is that all orders are literally phoned in from telephones stationed at each booth. Calls go into a central switchboard, where they are processed.

In addition to bringing in a booming family business, the motorized, choo-choo-like gizmo serves a practical function, according to Kropf. As was originally intended, it helps cut down labor costs by about 10 percent.

As Kropf explained, "My father owned a drive-in, and whenever the weather turned bad, the problem he always faced was curb hops calling in sick." But by the time Fred (Fritz) Kropf Sr. finally figured out how to solve his staffing woes with an automated delivery system, eight years had elapsed and the neighborhood hosting the drive-in had deteriorated. With some minor modifications, he was able to adapt his invention to his new sit-down establishment, Fritz's.

In all the years that the equipment has been operating, Kropf reports few mechanical breakdowns—aside from an occasional bowl of chili that accidentally dumps on a customer.

Servers bring out the beverages. "We try to keep service real personable," said Kropf.

There is no separate children's menu, though kids tend to order the "Round House Special." The hamburger-fries-small drink deal sells for $2.65 and is delivered in a cardboard carton covered with

Mickey Mouse or Teenage Mutant Ninja Turtle contact paper. Grown-ups, meanwhile, prefer the "Gen Dare." At $1.95, it's a hamburger patty with grilled onions and hash browns sprinkled in melted cheese, all sandwiched in a seeded bun.

# Chapter Three

# *Marketing from the Menu*

Menus sell food. They also set the mood, capture the image of an operation, create an impression, and convey a theme. The trend in children's menus is to go even further—to entertain, amuse, and stimulate imaginative minds while keeping little hands occupied until food arrives.

Are separate children's menus necessary? If youngsters are infrequent guests or their visits amount to a small percentage of business, then perhaps it is possible to get away without one. Training staff to inform guests of the availability of half-orders may suffice.

However, if the goal is to establish immediate rapport with families then the question deserves an affirmative answer. Setting down a special placemat or menu makes children feel welcome and parents feel wanted. The dining room is under control and you're able to go about the primary business of putting food on the table.

Given the many functions that children's menus must perform, there are a number of factors to take into consideration when developing this mighty marketing tool.

## MENU OPTIONS

Banger Smith, vice president of The Menu Workshop in Seattle, Washington, is of the opinion that flashy, four-color kids' menus are a detraction rather than an attraction to young customers. "It amazes me that restaurants go to the expense of producing four-color printed pieces," he said. "Use some color, but leave a lot of room for kids to be creative."

"The trend of the moment is to create interactive menus which involve children, and keep them quiet while waiting for food," added Filet Menus' Marcia Petersen, director of projects of the Los Angeles, California firm. Paper placemats, designed for one-time use, then easily disposed of or taken home as souvenirs, are gaining acceptance around the country.

Cost is definitely a factor in the paper placemat's favor. They're a bargain compared to cover-bound menus printed on heavy stock paper. Plus, if children make a mistake or spill their soda and turn the entire tabletop into a soggy mess, the placemats are easily replaced.

"Absorbing sounds and picking up miscellaneous particles of food are the actual functions of placemats," said Petersen. "When they are customized to match a restaurant's decor or theme, they contribute to the ambience of the restaurant. Most important, they help operators market certain parts of their menu, such as their children's section.

"They're a great marketing tool since they sit in front of the customer throughout the duration of the meal."

## IDENTIFYING THE AUDIENCE

Whatever format the menu takes, its content should be targeted. The needs of a toddler, who may be content to scribble on a paper napkin, contrast sharply with a five-, six-, or seven-year-old seeking greater challenges. Neither group compares to tweens, ages 10 to 12, whose tastes in tabletop activities are much more advanced (after all, they can read!) and tastes in food are somewhat more sophisticated than their younger siblings'.

The great majority of children's menus cut off kids at 12 years old. However, there is a growing movement to lower the age bracket to those 10 and under.

"Older kids prefer ordering appetizers or half-portions off the adult menu," said Smith. Why? After meeting with a group of fourth-graders (nine- and 10-year-olds) to talk about menus, the conclusion was, "It's cooler."

Big kids versus little kids, boys versus girls all have special interests. Since it would be a logistical nightmare (and too costly a proposition) to create age-specific, sex-specific menus, "I recommend having something for everyone," said Smith. "Gear half the games to those six and under, with the remainder designed for those six to 10."

## FUN AND GAMES

Arm tots with crayons (packed in a box or small wax paper bag or placed on the table in a juice glass holder), and set them to work on various projects. Here are some interactive ideas (involving both parents and offspring) that serve as fillers on menus and placemats and are designed to make time really fly.

- Pictures to color. Tie in to seasons, current social or pop trends, or restaurant themes (sombreros, piñatas, a chart of chile peppers for a Mexican restaurant; a map of Italy, pasta shapes, cannoli, or a scoop of spumoni for an Italian restaurant; Indians, cowboys, horses, ribs on a grill at a barbecue restaurant).

- Complete the picture (a pizza crust or hot dog or hamburger bun to fill in; ice cream in a dish to transform into a sundae).

- Fill in the frame with a self- or family portrait, a favorite food, a birthday or holiday wish. (This is a great way for those on tight budgets to stimulate creativity. Just draw a box on a page, and encourage kids to let their imaginations run wild.)

- Connect the dots, moving from number to number or letter to letter.

- Hidden word and unscramble the letters games, taking items directly off the children's menu.

- Simple crossword puzzles, again incorporating items from the menu.
- Find the hidden pictures game, if possible depicting a family dining scene.
- Find the picture that doesn't belong game.
- Tic-tac-toe boards.
- Mazes.

Fun facts, jokes, and riddles are also popular pastimes:

*Child*: Dad, will you remember me in one year?

*Dad*: Yes.

*Child*: Will you remember me in two years?

*Dad*: Yes.

*Child*: Will you remember me in three years?

*Dad*: Yes.

*Child*: Will you remember me in four, five, six, seven, eight, nine, and ten years?

*Dad*: Yes. Yes. Yes. Yes. Yes. Yes. And yes.

*Child*: Knock. Knock.

*Dad*: Who's there?

*Child*: See, you forgot me already!

## PRICING STRATEGIES

Less is more when it comes to pricing items on children's menus. In this value-conscious age, a minimal charge for a child's meal translates into a tremendous benefit for those tightly controlling purse strings. By sacrificing short-run profits, hopefully, more customers will be beating on the door and long-term loyalties will be established.

How low are you willing to go to satisfy price-sensitive parents?

Slash prices from the adult menu in half. Position items at the break-even point. Have children pay what they weigh. Take their age, times 50 cents. Keep dinners under $5, under $3, at $1.95. How about letting kids eat free one day a week? Four days a week? Every day of the week? For an entire month? These are just some of the ways to resolve the issue of what to charge—or what not to charge.

The fact that it doesn't cost a lot of money to eat at Chili's Bar & Grill is one reason why the chain has become such a popular family destination, according to Ron McDougall, president of parent company Brinker International, Dallas, Texas. "The family market goes to the basic positioning of our concept," McDougall said. "Why go to Chili's? Because it doesn't take a lot of time. Booth seating hides the kids. So you don't see them. We have just enough noise level. So you don't hear them either. And we keep prices down."

## THE FOOD FACTOR

When a major hotel chain decided it was time to add healthy choices to its children's menu, a dozen food consultants flew in from all parts of the country to participate in a taste testing. The panel of experts assembled at corporate headquarters to yea or nay whether good-for-you food could be good tasting too.

Convened around a table, their feet barely reaching the floor, they were served the first course. "Turkey Burgers" elicited 24 thumbs up.

The next order of business, "Crispy Chicken Nuggets," didn't fly as well. The panel okayed the chicken that had been coated in whole grain cereal and baked instead of fried, but they nixed the salsa that came on the side.

Reaction was also mixed to "Power Pita Pizza," with the consensus being to add more low-fat cheese and turkey meat sausage, and get rid of the mushrooms and onions.

The input of the youth council, ages seven to 13, proved invaluable in creating the "Cuisine Naturelle" items that eventually made it onto Hyatt Hotels' "Camp Hyatt Happy Campers" menu, according to Julie Halpern, director of special projects. "Kids are savvy and sophisticated. They definitely have opinions and they gave us great comments—after we told them that our chefs wouldn't be offended if they didn't like something."

Certainly, a focus group made up of kids is one way to test selections, generate immediate feedback, and zero in on the foods that appeal most to this target market. By listening to customers, observing their ordering patterns, and consulting with waitstaff, it is also possible to get a good handle on children's favorite foods.

The National Restaurant Association provides additional insight. In the report *The Market for Children and Family Dining* adults surveyed ranked the top five favorite foods for children under age six as:

- Hamburgers
- French fries
- Chicken
- Spaghetti
- Hot dogs
- Pizza

Not surprising, according to adults, children ages six to 12 prefer similar foods in slightly different order:

- Hamburgers
- Chicken
- French fries
- Pizza
- Fish and chips tied with steak

All children under 18 also appear to be increasing their consumption of Mexican and Oriental items, according to NPD CREST.

## DO PLAY WITH FOOD

To give children the foods they want, and at the same time, develop dishes that set operations apart, it is possible to take tried-and-true favorites and vary the theme. (Hyatt accomplished this very feat by giving a healthy slant to burgers, fried chicken, and pizza.)

- Instead of one big burger, offer mini-burgers on mini-buns.
- Add a slice of mozzarella to hamburger patties, brush a toasted bun with pizza sauce, and offer "pizza burgers" with a choice of toppings (onion rings, crushed bacon, fresh tomato slices).
- For "Sloppy Jose," add mild salsa to chopped, ground beef. Serve the prepared mixture on a bun, in a pita pocket, or rolled in a corn or flour tortilla, with chopped lettuce, chopped tomato, and grated cheese on the side.
- Split hot dogs lengthwise and stuff with cheese (American or mild cheddar). Wrap with bacon, then grill or broil until the hot dog is heated through, the bacon is cooked, and the cheese is melted for a delicious "Swankie Frankie" (a personal favorite from my past).
- Another way to dress up dogs is to wrap them in puff pastry or bagel dough, then bake. Serve with catsup and mustard "dipping sauces."
- Peel and thinly slice potatoes. Using a cookie cutter, transform the slices into fun shapes; then bake or fry them. For convenience, frozen alphabet fries are now on the market as are fish nuggets in seaworthy shapes. (Check Sources.)
- Creative pizza ideas include arranging toppings to simulate a face, cutting out dough in animal shapes, or making a "Mickey Mouse Pizza," a specialty of Spago in West Hollywood, California. Chef-proprietor Wolfgang Puck prepares and bakes two small cheese pizzas, then cuts one in half to produce two mouse ears that are positioned at the top of the

whole pizza. Use slices of ripe olives for eyes, a mushroom for the nose, and a sliced tomato for the smiling mouth.

- Other pizza treats include pita pizzas, breakfast pizzas (an open-faced English muffin topped with bacon, ham, or sausage and eggs), and dessert pizzas (cream cheese on a baked pizza round, topped with apple, pear, plum, or peach slices or berries, depending on the season).

- Shells, wheels, corkscrews, bow ties, and radiators are pasta shapes that are easier—and more fun—to eat than traditional spaghetti.

- To enhance the value of sandwiches, build up such standards as grilled cheese and PB&J into triple-decker delights.

- On the subject of peanut butter, in addition to jelly, other popular complements include banana or apple slices, crumbled bacon, raisins, shredded carrots, and honey.

- For accompaniments or garnishes to center-of-the-plate fare, consider carrot curls, vegetable and fruit kabobs, apple fans, melon wedges, and grape clusters. (When Walt Disney World Resort began offering grapes as a substitute for french fries with sandwiches, Keith Keogh, Epcot Center's executive chef, reported that kids chose the fruit 15 to 20 percent of the time.)

## PREPARATION TIPS

Here are some general guidelines to follow when preparing children's meals.

- Keep a ceiling on seasonings. While the adult population is growing increasingly fond of spicier flavors, children's taste buds are still at a highly sensitive stage of development. Keep preparations as plain (i.e., bland) as possible.

- Along with spices, fresh herbs should be avoided. Although they may immensely improve the flavor of grilled or roasted chicken, fish, seafood, and ground beef-based dishes, to a child chopped herbs are just "yucky chunks of green stuff" that must be eliminated from the plate.

- Presentation counts when courting kids. Don't overload them with more food than they can possibly eat. In fact, portions should be kept small, manageable, easy to handle, appetizing. The United States Department of Agriculture's daily recommendations for children two to 10 are two- to three-ounce portions of cooked meat, fish, and poultry, and for teens, four- to five-ounce portions.

- Offer finger foods. "Children like to use their hands when they eat. They like to be active and get involved," said National Restaurant Association staff nutritionist Diane Welland. Items that they can put together, such as fajitas, are good choices. Other "fun foods" include chicken and beef kebabs (to serve after removing skewers), drumsticks and chicken wings, fresh vegetables and dips, stuffed potato skins, and corn on the cob.

- Mix at your own risk. It's much safer to serve dressings and sauces on the side.

- Avoid food that requires lengthy preparation. Mature diners can take the 45-minute wait for deep dish, Chicago-style pizza or baked-to-order soufflés. Children are another story. Upon ordering, they want to eat immediately, if not sooner.

- Serve food that is ready to eat. Butter toast. On salads, cut tomatoes, cucumbers, and carrots into bite-sized pieces. Cut up meat, when possible. Serve sandwiches sliced in thirds or quarters. Ask how the child would like his or her hot dog or hamburger, and apply condiments in the kitchen.

- Be conscious of temperature. Never bring out sizzling hot food on plates or bowls that have sat too long under heat lamps.

- Break traditions during meal periods. Consider starting the day with grilled cheese sandwiches, peanut butter, cottage cheese/cinnamon/raisins on toast. Or how about breakfast bowls of soup? At lunch and dinner, popular selections include pancakes, cereal with yogurt and fresh fruit, and mini-bagels with cream cheese and jelly.

## MENU OBJECTIVES

"Children's meals should truly satisfy children," said James McNeal, an expert in marketing to children. "Just as they love to feel the rough bark as they slide down a tree and mud oozing between their toes, they love food of all different textures—food that mushes in their mouth as well as food that is tough to chew. In addition to tasting, aroma is especially important to children. Their olfactory system needs a lot of exercise.

"To really please children, meals must have some play value. It doesn't have to cost more. Creative effort is all that it takes."

If you agree that fun is a major ingredient too often missing from children's meals, the question is: What are fun foods? Any items that can be picked up and eaten with fingers, and that come in silly shapes. You probably already stock a variety of foods that fit this description. There are also specific products now on the market targeted specifically for children. (See Sources.) In many cases, a minor alteration in presentation will create a brand-new specialty dish that will earn raves from kid critics. Some suggestions:

- Chicken nuggets shaped like lips or hearts
- Fish nuggets in assorted sea shapes
- Toppings on pizza to resemble faces or animal figures
- Squiggles of mustard and catsup on a hot dog
- Ribbons of cream or yogurt in a cream-based soup
- Pasta in any shape other than spaghetti and linguine
- Sandwiches cut into geometric forms or animal figures using cookie cutters
- Tomato roses, cucumber and carrot ribbons, apple swans
- Curly Q fries

- Mashed potatoes piped into floral patterns
- Ice cream scooped in a dish, and then topped with two chocolate wafers to create Mickey Mouse ears
- Blue gelatin with fish-shaped fruit chews served in a glass or glass bowl (to resemble an aquarium)

## WHAT'S AHEAD

The portfolio of children's menus on the pages that follow provides additional food for thought. Use this window of opportunity to find out what constitutes successful "sell pieces." Then, take what you've seen and learned. Begin formulating ideas of your own on how to get the most mileage from the vehicle that connects customers to the kitchen.

## MENUS PAST AND PRESENT

In the 1950s and 1960s, some years before highways were lined with golden arches, turquoise blue and orange beacons lured customers by the carloads. This was the heyday of Howard Johnson's, a chain of roadside restaurants that tempted travelers from coast to coast with "good food at sensible prices" and 28 different flavors of ice cream.

HoJo's was also one of the first chains to corner the family market, scoring major points with minors by treating them to their own special menus. Some of the earliest offerings tied into its Simple Simon and the Pieman trademark, and included the "Humpty Dumpty Lunch" (small chicken salad, bread and butter, fresh strawberry ice cream, and milk for 70 cents); the "Simple Simon Special" (broiled lamb chop, fresh vegetable and potato, bread and butter, ice cream and cookie, milk or hot chocolate for 95 cents); and the "Peter Piper Plate" (cup of soup, mashed potato with gravy, fresh peas with butter, bread and butter, small ice cream, milk or hot chocolate for 60 cents). That was back in the days when a la carte children's items included "Milk Toast" for 20 cents and an ice cream cone for 10 cents.

Over the years, menus began satisfying the dual purpose of listing food as well as keeping kids occupied with activities, stories, games, puzzles, and fold-outs. Prices gradually rose and the offerings altered to reflect changing tastes. But the creative titles of kids' meals, which had become somewhat of a signature, remained. Spaghetti with Italian-style tomato sauce was called "Mr. Twist." Fried clams went by "Super Sailor." And the ever-popular grilled hot dog on a toasted, buttered bun became "Fearless Fido."

Fast forward to the present. There are now just over 100 Howard Johnson restaurants, compared to a high of 1,040 in 1979, according to Barbara Leveroni, vice president of support services of Franchise Associates, Inc., the South Weymouth, Massachusetts management and marketing company owned and operated by Howard Johnson's restaurant franchisees. Families are definitely still courted, but kids' menus are admittedly scaled down compared to those issued in years past. (See Figure 3–1.)

Instead of costly die-cut printed pieces, a four-page booklet of games and activities suffices. "We just don't have the ability to print as many as we used to," said Leveroni.

In designing menus today, three guidelines are followed:

1. Keep it simple.
2. Target kids under 10.
3. Keep costs down so the menu can be a giveaway.

Clever wording of kids' meals is also missing. Now the children of children who grew up on "Spreadie Freddie" (peanut butter and jelly sandwich) and "Plymouth Rocky" (sliced roast turkey), washed down with HoJo Cola, are presented with a selection of tell-it-like-it-is items—from fried fish fillets and chicken fingers to spaghetti and meatballs, macaroni and cheese, and fried clams, all priced at $3.50. The standard cheeseburger, hot dog, and grilled cheese, with french fries and a beverage, are also available at $2.75.

"We also print four to six coloring sheets a year, which are geared to the seasons and holidays," said Leveroni. "We invite kids to decorate them, and bring them back on their next visit. They always get a free ice cream cone for turning them in. Some restaurants do drawings for bikes or savings bonds."

## MENU WITH A MESSAGE

At Phoenix, Arizona-based Ramada Hotels, radiating across the United States and into Canada, children are fed facts on world ecology along with a listing of their favorite foods. (See Figure 3–2.)

The special children's menu, featured in hotel restaurants as well as in guest rooms, is shaped like a suitcase. Attached to the handle, where a luggage tag ordinarily hangs, is an entry form to fill out and redeem for a free birthday meal. On the front are colorful animal illustrations. As eager readers learn on the back of the menu, four of the six featured species are endangered.

To find out food listings, it is necessary to flip open each animal's mouth. On the tip of the hippo's tongue is written "A Hefty Hamburger on a Bun with French Fries." The alligator advertises "Our Snappy Grilled Cheese Sandwich with French Fries." The lion's choice is "The Roar of Fried Chicken Drumsticks with Mashed Potatoes, Gravy, and Roll." Opening the gorilla's mouth reveals "A Tangle of Spaghetti with Meat Sauce." The panda promotes "Fruit-Faced Pancakes or Waffle with Whipped Cream." And the humpback whale spouts "Ice Cream Swimming Beneath Hot Fudge or Caramel Topping."

"We've taken foods that really appeal to children, and tried to give families something that they could have fun with," said Stephen Beehag, vice president of food and beverages, North America, who was instrumental in the menu design.

Five different ways to save the earth and five different things to do to save endangered species are listed on the back. There is also a jungle scene to color, with a message underneath that reads, "This menu helped save a tree! It's printed on recycled paper."

# KIDS GO HOJO

## for Kids 10 and under
All Kids Meals include a choice of beverage
• Milk • Chocolate Milk • Apple Juice • Pepsi•

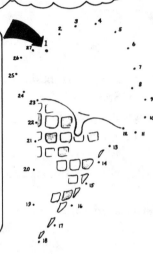

## BREAKFAST
### Kids pick your favorite 2.95

1. Two Hot Cakes with one sausage pattie.
2. One Egg with strip of bacon and toast.
3. *Kellogg's*® cold cereal or **QUAKER**® oatmeal with banana and milk and an English muffin.

*Where available*
**All-You-Can-Eat Breakfast Bar**
½ price   or under 5 — FREE *(with adult purchase)*

## LUNCH or DINNER
### Served with fries...except items 4, 5 and 6

| | | | | | |
|---|---|---|---|---|---|
| 1. | HOJO Pizza | 3.50 | 6. | Roast Turkey | 3.50 |
| 2. | Fried Fish Fillets | 3.50 | 7. | Fried Clams | 3.50 |
| 3. | Chicken Fingers | 3.50 | 8. | Cheeseburger | 2.75 |
| 4. | Spaghetti & Meatballs | 3.50 | 9. | Hot Dog | 2.75 |
| 5. | Macaroni & Cheese | 3.50 | 10. | Grilled Cheese | 2.75 |

*Where available*
**All-You-Can-Eat Salad Bar**
½ price   or under 5 — FREE *(with adult purchase)*

...And for **DESSERT** Your Choice .95

■ Howard Johnson's famous Ice Cream
■ Junior Size Sundae  ■ Jell-O®  ■ Yogurt

Figure 3-1   Howard Johnson kids' menu (courtesy of Franchise Associates, Inc., South Weymouth, MA)

# TRY THESE GAMES

**Y**ou can build at least 12 words from these letters — see if you can find these words...

3 Girl's Names _____ _____ _____

3 Boy's Names _____ _____ _____

3 Animals _____ _____ _____

3 Vegetables _____ _____ _____

(are there any more words?) _____ _____ _____

Clue! You can use a letter more than once.

C N B S R O A D P J T E L

ANSWERS: Carol, Jean, Rose. Bob, Peter, Don. Cat, Bear, Leopard. Beets, Peas, Carrots

Look closely at these things....then find the same things — but drawn in a different position! Connect them with a line—*look carefully they're all there!*

MY NAME IS: _____

I LIVE IN: _____

I AM _____ YEARS OLD

PRINTED IN U.S.A. ON RECYCLED PAPER

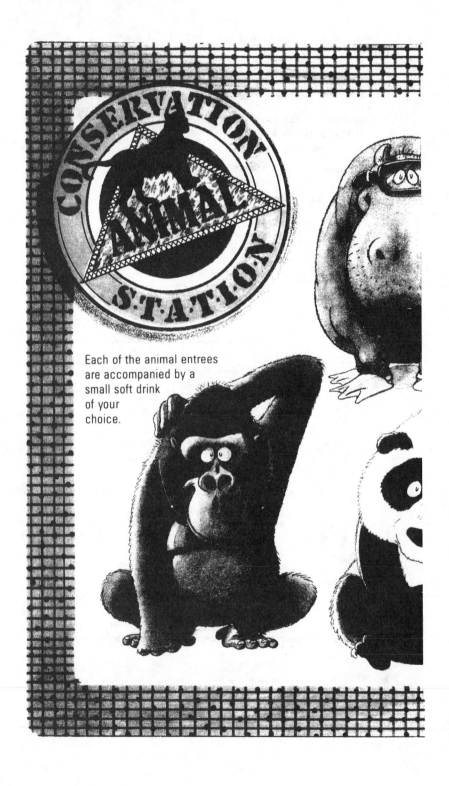

Each of the animal entrees
are accompanied by a
small soft drink
of your
choice.

# THINGS YOU CAN DO TO SAVE ENDANGERED ANIMALS

**1** Don't buy anything made of wild animal skins. Like a rug made from a zebra. Or a wallet made from a seal.

**2** Learn how to identify endangered animals. Did you know four out of six animals on the right are endangered? Can you tell which ones they are?

**3** Adopt an endangered animal. Maybe a baby gorilla. Or panda. To adopt an animal, you give the zoo money to take care of it. Ask a grown-up to help you. Or get together with a bunch of friends.

**4** Become an endangered animal "expert." Read books about these animals. Watch nature shows on TV. Ask grown-ups to plan a trip to the zoo.

**5** Be careful with helium-filled balloons. Did you know they can hurt animals? If these balloons blow out to sea, turtles and whales can swallow them. And that's very, very bad. So hang on to those balloons. Don't let them blow away!

**Lucky Lion**
"G-r-r-r!" he says. "I'm not in danger." Lions are lucky. They have families to help them hunt. They stick together, hunt together, settle down to a good meal. But what if there's nothing left to hunt?

**Happy Hippo**
The full name is hippopotamus. It means river horse. Isn't the hippo a funny-looking horse with those short legs? Hippos live near rivers, eat plants. There's plenty of food. For now.

**Anxious Alligator**
Alligators should be nervous. There are not too many left in America. People used to make shoes with their hides. How silly! Would you want alligator shoes? They might start nibbling on your toes!

**Poor Panda**
Does the zoo near you have a panda? Yes! You're lucky. Many zoos don't. There are so few pandas in the world. In China, their food supply is disappearing. Pandas really need help.

**Worried Whale**
They're big. S-o-o-o big, some whales could fill an entire block. And they have such wonderful names. Humpback. Finback. Bowhead. But watch out. These whales are in danger of disappearing forever.

**Groaning Gorilla**
"Oh, no!" he says. And scratches his head. He can't understand why he's endangered. It's not right! He's such a gentle, shy giant.

**FRIENDS OF THE EARTH**

*Every day, in some small way, let's help our animal friends "stay."*

Figure 3-2 Ramada Hotel kids' menu (courtesy of Ramada Hotels, Phoenix, AZ)

## NEW AGE FOOD FOR ALL AGES

Late for the Train in Menlo Park, California, has been a whole foods haven since 1977. The 120-seat restaurant serves only organic fruits and vegetables, fresh fish, seafood, and poultry. Everything is prepared from scratch, including baked goods made of organic grains and flours. With no burgers, no processed meats, no white bread on the menu, there's NO WAY children will frequent this place.

WAY.

"We really cater to families," said restaurant spokesperson Jahanna Tafari. "At brunch on the weekends, we'll do 500 covers a day. A large majority of them are children."

Dinner also is a draw for people of all ages pursuing a diet free of preservatives, additives, and processed foods. On the children's menu, which is decorated with authentic kid masterpieces, meals fall in the $6 range compared to $9.95 to $14.95 for full-portion, center-of-the-plate fare. Popular offerings include spinach fettucine with butter or Alfredo sauce; fresh fish; grilled chicken strips; chicken breast strips that are breaded with pecans, then fried in safflower oil; and tofu, which is grilled until firm and served with pineapple and ginger. All entrees are accompanied by steamed vegetables, usually a mélange of carrots, broccoli, cauliflower, and spinach.

"Very rarely do kids not eat what they're served," said Tafari.

A toy chest in the waiting area has also been a real boon to family business. The box is stocked with building blocks, playing cards, crayons, and coloring books.

## THE HIGH ROAD TO SUCCESS

New York City streets and avenues are lined with restaurants catering to every taste and pocketbook, with cuisines ranging from Afghan to Vietnamese (according to *Zagat Restaurant Survey*). But it's the Boulevard, an American restaurant specializing in barbecue, that attracts families with children.

"It's idiotic, but there are many places in this city that discourage kids," said owner Stewart Rosen. "In response to customers' requests, we started a kids' menu, and it's made the restaurant successful."

The Upper West Side establishment lists seven entrees on its "Little Monster's Menu." (See Figure 3–3.) All are served with choice of beverage and a scoop of ice cream, and sell for $5.95.

"We wanted to have something from every food group that kids would eat," Rosen said. He added that the items are priced as loss leaders. But adults in the company of their kids order too, which ultimately helps pump up the bottom line.

Heavy traffic also contributes to offsetting the lower check averages that often result when children are part of the dining party. Over a typical week, the 160-seat restaurant turns out approximately 600 kids' meals.

Tiny tykes are presented with a selection of favorite stand-bys, prepared specifically to their liking (such as "Grilled Cheese on Wonder Bread"). And some of the items' names have been changed to instill greater importance (such as "Bratburger" for hamburger, "Sketties and Red Gravy" for spaghetti and tomato sauce).

For those who don't have time to dine in the restaurant, the entire children's menu is also available for takeout.

## ANCHORS AWEIGH

Royal Caribbean Cruises Ltd. has a reputation for being the champagne cruise line. As more children come aboard, the luxury fleet is also gaining renown as the Shirley Temple of ships.

In mid-1991 a full-scale dining program designed just for kids was implemented to accommodate guests' requests. The menu is a central element, featured in an eight-page activity book entitled "Captain Sealy's Kids' Galley." (See Figure 3–4.)

There are four different versions of the book, which are printed at the same time to save money. All share the same four-color cover and dedicate the center spread to menu listings. What changes are the four black-and-white activity pages.

## MONSTER'S MENU

served with milk or soda
and a scoop of ice cream

Bratburger with Fries
◆
Sketties and Red Gravy
◆
Hot Doggie and Fries
◆
Grilled Cheese on Wonder Bread
◆
Chicken Fingers with
BBQ Sauce and Fries
◆
Rascal's Ribs
with Mashed Potatoes
◆
Ten Veg Fried Rice

### 5.95

## FREE DELIVERY AVAILABLE

*Mon-Sun 5:30 pm to 10:30 pm*
*West 79th Street to West 95th Street*
*Riverside to Columbus*
*Minimum Order: $10*
*All major credit cards accepted*

## 2398 BROADWAY AT 88TH ST
## 212◆874◆7400

Figure 3-3 "Little Monsters" menu (courtesy of Boulevard, New York, NY)

Figure 3-4  Kids' activity book and menu (courtesy of Royal Caribbean Cruises Ltd., Miami, FL)

In determining what to serve, extensive research was conducted, according to Alice Rodriguez, menu coordinator of the Miami, Florida-based operation. "We came to the conclusion that kids as well as parents on vacation really don't want to worry about getting all their vitamins, eating really healthy foods," she said. "They also do not like nouvelle cuisine or anything too gourmet.

"So we came up with a children's menu featuring all the foods kids like."

Hot dogs and hamburgers, however, proved to be a hard sell to top chefs manning the gourmet galleys. They recommended a more upscale selection. Rodriguez countered with, "Trust me, I'm a mother." Then a compromise was reached to assure that every selection on the children's menu met Royal Caribbean's standards for quality and consistency.

"We're not going to give them processed food," said Rodriguez.

Chicken noodle and chicken alphabet soups are made from scratch. The tuna fish sandwich is actually prepared with salmon mousse. For the minute steak sandwich, butchers on board cut six-ounce sirloins. "Captain Hook's Fish Fingers" are prepared with fresh fillets of fish.

The menus are available for lunch and dinner in each ship's dining room. A buffet, featuring hot dogs, hamburgers, barbequed ribs, and other kiddie food favorites, is also served at lunch in each ship's cafe.

## FRISBEE MEALS FLY

When both mom and dad work outside the home, coordinating a vacation is quite a job. The simplest solution is to take short getaways, as often as possible, and to bring along the kids.

"We're seeing a lot more working parents opt for four- and five-day vacations," said Ken Halligan, food and beverage director of The Westin La Paloma in Tucson, Arizona. "Children are an integral part of their travel plans, and they've become important customers for us."

The 487-room property now offers separate children's menus in all five of its dining facilities.

"Errol Finn" is the mascot in La Villa, a restaurant specializing in fish and seafood. The signature sea creature, touting a beanie and riding a skateboard, appears on a tabletop card listing an array of golden oldies and contemporary hits. The selection includes chicken fingers, pasta with red or white sauce, and fish and seafood kebabs that string on a stick chunks of tuna, swordfish, salmon, and shrimp.

"You'd be amazed how many kids like shrimp," said Halligan. "We sauté four jumbo shrimp, and serve them on rice with broccoli. We don't add any seasonings. Children aren't fussy that way." Halligan added, "The only seasoning they do prefer comes out of a bottle" (as in catsup).

In the Dessert Garden, a casual restaurant at the Westin La Paloma serving three meals a day, the children's menu is printed on a white 8.5" × 11" paper bag. (See Figure 3–5.) The characters "Sabino Sam," a barbecue king of a coyote, and his rabbit buddy adorn the cover. The line art was commissioned by a local company. But lettering appears to have been done by a child, who has a tendency to write "s" and "e" backwards.

New York steak, at $8.50, is the priciest item on the menu. All other offerings—from "Kid Pasta" to "Kid Sandwich" to "Kid Chicken Tenders"—fall in the $2.00 to $3.00 range, and include salad or "Cup of Day Soup." The entrees are served on nine-inch plates.

However, at the poolside cafe, kids' meals fly out of the kitchen on frisbees bearing the resort's logo. "They've been a real hit," said Halligan.

"As we became aware of the importance of children, our marketing efforts got a lot more aggressive," he added. "Reservations, the front desk, the restaurants, have all come together to promote our kids' programs."

Now as soon as families check in, children receive a coupon redeemable for a free slushie drink at the pool. Another coupon is good for a pizza party, available through room service, featuring an

## BREAKFAST

| | |
|---|---|
| Kid Eggs & Bacon . . . . . . . . . . . | $2.50 |
| Kid Cereal . . . . . . . . . . . . . | $1.50 |
| Kid French Toast . . . . . . . . . | $2.50 |
| Kid Pancakes . . . . . . . . . . . . | $2.50 |

### *Includes Choice of Juice

## LUNCH & DINNER

| | |
|---|---|
| Kid Pasta . . . . . . . . . . . . . | $2.00 |
| Kid New York Steak . . . . . . . . | $8.50 |
| Kid Hot Dog . . . . . . . . . . . . | $3.00 |
| Kid Hamburger . . . . . . . . . . . | $3.00 |
| Kid Sandwich . . . . . . . . . . | $2.50 |
| Kid Chicken Tenders . . . . . . . | $3.00 |

### *All Dinners Served With Salad or Cup of Day Soup

## THE WESTIN LA PALOMA

Figure 3-5   Paper bag children's menu, The Dessert Garden (courtesy of the Westin La Paloma, Tucson, AZ)

11-inch pizza, a bag of chips, and four drinks. In total, it's a $12 value.

The Westin La Paloma also runs the "Kactus Kids' Klub," offering day-long activities for children six and under, six to 12, and 12 to 16.

## BRAND NAME CHARACTERS BOLSTER FAMILY BUSINESS

Denny's entrance in the children's market dates back to 1988, when the Flintstones' license was acquired.

"Family restaurants were changing. We were attracting more and more children. And that presented us with an opportunity," said Susan Schneider, marketing manager of the Spartanburg, South Carolina-based chain. The initial push to slice off a greater share of the kids' pie was with plush toys—of Fred Flintstone, Barney Rubble, and their families—which went on sale at Denny's check-out counters nationwide.

"It was a self-liquidating promotion. The cost of the premium was passed on to consumers in the price of the toys," said Schneider. "So Denny's costs were covered."

By the fall of 1990 a special menu for children 10 and under was introduced, featuring "Bedrock Breakfast Favorites" and "Flintstones Fun Meals" for lunch and dinner dayparts. A Flintstones toy was included with each purchase.

Still working with Hanna-Barbera after the Flintstones license expired, Denny's propelled into the Space Age with the Jetsons. (See Figure 3–6.) The items listed and featured in four-color on the brand-new menu remained basically the same, but names changed. "French Slamasaurus Jr." turned into "Futuristic French Toast." Pancakes that were "Prehistoric" became "Planetary." The "Corn Dogosaurus" was replaced with the "Meteoric Space Doggie." "Sabertooth Chicken Basket" went "Cosmic" while the "Glacier Sundae" went "Atomic."

"To keep kids busy and get parents more involved, we developed an educational activity book to include with the menu," said

Figure 3-6 Denny's "The Jetson's" kids' menu (courtesy of Denny's, Spartanburg, SC)

**Lunch Dinner**

### Atomic Sundae
Chocolate, Hot Fudge or
Strawberry Sundae .85

### Shooting Star Shrimp Basket
Six pieces of delicious deep-fried shrimp,
served with fries and a roll. 2.70

### Big Dipper Beverages
Milk, Juice, Soft Drinks, Lemonade .55
Hot Chocolate .75

### Cosmic Chicken Basket
Two all-white meat chicken fillet strips,
served with fries and a roll. 2.70

### Meteoric Space Doggie!
One hot dog, served in a basket with fries.
2.35
with cheese 2.45

**For children 10 and under**

Schneider. "The 12 pages of stories, puzzles, games, and fun facts revolve around the space theme."

Rather than developing signature cartoon figures, Denny's had the resources, and good reasons, to acquire licensed characters.

"It was decided to tie into well-known brand names to gain immediate recognition, and help make it easier for kids to decide where to eat," Schneider said.

"Families are aware of the Flintstones and now the Jetsons. They are popular. And they are affordable compared to Disney characters."

## EAT 'N PLAY

"We are more interested in serving children well than looking at them as a profit center," said Basil Cox, executive vice president of Eat 'n Park. So when it came time to develop a children's menu, the 54-unit family restaurant chain came up with a selection of breakfast through dinner items priced well below $2.00.

The next step was to approach its Pittsburgh, Pennsylvania neighbor, Family Communications, Inc. The child experts and producers of public television's popular program, "Mister Rogers' Neighborhood," were presented with a double-edged challenge: to find a way to keep kids busy and to involve parents as well in the 10- to 15-minute period between being seated and being served.

Freshmen in the field of foodservice, Family Communications brought a new perspective to menu planning, eventually delivering a totally original communication vehicle designed to drive forward interaction between grown-ups and children.

The earliest work consisted of a series of 2″ × 3″ "Flip Books." (See Figure 3–7.) Flip through the pages one way to find a complete animated story. Then, turn the book upside down and over to find mini-pages filled with descriptions and illustrations of all items available for "special guests under 12." (For those too young to read, pictures of plated presentations are worth more than words and a great way to engage young minds in the process of selecting what to eat.)

Figure 3-7    Flip book (courtesy of Eat 'n Park, Pittsburgh, PA)

According to Cathy Droz, project coordinator, the books were produced four at a time, with a lifespan expectancy of four to six months.

"Eat 'n Park gets a lot of return business. So it was good to change them," Droz said.

"Flip Books" evolved into "Flip Flap Menus." (See Figure 3–8.) Instructions printed on lively, four-color illustrated 5″ × 8″ cards encouraged children to lift up various flaps to find different pic-

**Figure 3-8    Flip flap menu (courtesy of Eat 'n Park, Pittsburgh, PA)**

tures. "That was very engaging for kids, like a game of peek-a-boo," said Droz. "To go through all the flaps, it took kids about 10 minutes—or even longer if an imaginative parent made a game out of it."

"Family Fun Fold-Ups" followed. (See Figure 3–9.) Items were listed on one side of the menu. On the back, in addition to word games and puzzles, were instructions on how to fold up the menu, place fingers under flaps, and configure it into three different scenes.

Year after year, the parade of clever and creative, wild and wonderful children's menus continued, according to Basil Cox.

"They were relatively elaborate and up there in cost," added Droz. "They were the gifts that we gave the children."

Today, Eat 'n Park still gives serious thought to its children's menus, but has adopted a much more practical approach. Kids are catered to with a paper menumat, featured on the flip side of placemats. (See Figure 3–10.) It's black-and-white and geared to a slightly younger audience, "special guests 10 and under." "Sparkle," a star-shaped mascot who appears only to children and "helps kids be the best of whatever they are," is featured in a four-panel cartoon strip that runs along the top of the mat. Also included are games and activities related to the strip's story line.

All the color is provided by children, who upon being seated, receive crayons inscribed with the Eat 'n Park logo. After the meal, they get another treat: a free "Smiley" sugar cookie.

Eight different menumats are printed at a time, with a new set coming out every six months.

"This is by far the simplest of all children's menus that we've done," said Cox. "But there is such tremendous play value in it. It allows children to be whatever they want to be."

"From an operator's standpoint, this is also the simplest menu to

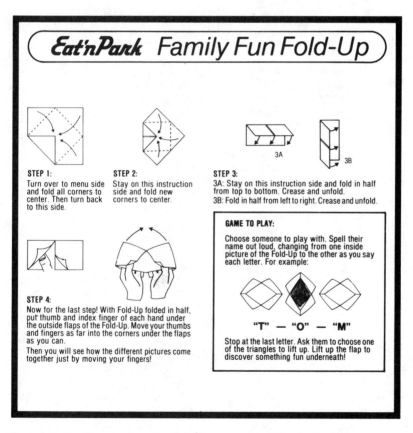

Figure 3-9   Family fun fold-up (courtesy of Eat 'n Park, Pittsburgh, PA)

## KIDS' MENU
### Eat'nPark

### For Our Special Guests 10 and Under

Baby food available at no charge on request. Children's menu items are not available for take-out.

#### BREAKFAST
Breakfast'n Fruit Buffet*
WEEKDAY SPECIAL $1.95
Weekends & Holidays $2.20
Sunday Brunch* $2.95
Hot or Cold Cereal with toast and juice $.95
Pancake, French Toast or
Waffle Special $1.45
Two pancakes or french toast or one waffle with two pieces of bacon or sausage.

Breakfast Special $1.30
One egg, two pieces of bacon or sausage, toast.

#### LUNCH'N DINNER
Lunch 'n Dinner side orders include:
French fries, fresh fruit, applesauce, cottage cheese, cole slaw, tossed salad and Jello*.

#### Sandwiches
Served with one side order of your choice.
Grilled Cheese $1.15   Hot Dog $.95
Hamburger $1.15   Cheeseburger $1.25
Pizza Boats™ $1.15

#### Dinners
Served with two side orders of your choice (one with Spaghetti) and a roll.
Breaded Chicken Fillets $2.25
Spaghetti with Meat Sauce $1.75
Boneless Fillet of Fish
Batter-dipped $1.95   Breaded $2.25

#### SOUP'N SALAD BAR*
Free for children under 5 with any adult Soup'n Salad Bar
With Lunch'n Dinner $.95
Soup'n Salad Bar Only $1.95

#### DESSERTS
Junior Sundae $.85   Jello* $.50
Dish of Ice Cream or Frozen Yogurt $.45
Berry, Fruit or Creme Pie $.95

#### DRINKS
Milk: White or Chocolate, Lemonade,
Soft Drink or Iced Tea $.55
Milkshake: Chocolate, Vanilla, Strawberry $1.15
*Where available

© 1990 EAT N PARK

## PICK THE PAIR
**Can you find the two flowers that are the same?**

**Planting flowers and trees helps keep the world healthy and beautiful.**

Figure 3-10   Menumat (menu side) (courtesy of Eat 'n Park, Pittsburgh, PA)

deliver," added Droz. "Instead of having to seat parties, go get children their menus, then return with them, hostesses now just flip over regular placemats and hand out crayons that are usually stashed in their apron pockets. They don't have to think about making extra trips to the table."

## MENU SPEAKS TO KIDS IN TWO LANGUAGES

Robin's in Pasadena, California, is an independent family restaurant with a reputation for being a "gastronomical toy store." While adults indulge in "Thermal Nuclear Hot Wings," "Japanese Noodle Chicken Salad," and "Garbage Burgers," kids get to choose from an equally eclectic menu. Offerings range from "Mini-Nachos with Cheese" (99 cents) to a "Little Porky Chick from Monterey" ($2.69), which is a scaled-down version of a grown-up's grilled chicken sandwich, to "REO Speed Wagon" ($1.79), a vanilla ice cream, chocolate, and Oreo cookie shake served with a red licorice straw.

On children's dining habits, owner Robin Salzer said, "We sell a lot of drumsticks because they are easier to pick up than chicken breast. We're also experimenting with corn dogs on a stick. Kids like all the basics, but their palates are getting more sophisticated. So we're also trying chicken with teriyaki sauce."

Aside from the selection, the physical appearance of the kid's menu makes it a stand out. (See Figure 3–11.) Laminated, day-glo colored paper is bound together in one easy-to-read volume that is written in two different languages—English and Spanish.

"After all, this is Southern California," said Salzer.

Young artists' illustrations add another dimension of interest to the layout while the plastic laminated pages make for easy cleanup. Plus, rounding out the breakfast, lunch, and dinner listings are pages describing how to sign up for the birthday club and how to qualify for a free chocolate sundae (by bringing in an "A" report card). One page also spells out the offer of free baby food for infants and toddlers.

"Our main focus is on families," said Salzer. Recognizing that a menu alone won't make the restaurant their number one destina-

# KID'S MENU

# MENU PARA NIÑOS

For all Robin's pals ages 12 & under.

Para los amigos de Robin's menores de 12 años.

Figure 3-11    English-Spanish kids' menu (courtesy of Robin's, Pasadena, CA)

# DINNER

Served after 11:00 a.m., Sunday at Noon

# CENA

Se serve despues de las 11:00 a.m., El Domingo en latarde

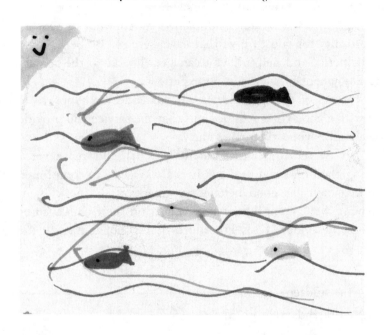

| Includes a kid's chocolate sundae | Incluso una nieve de chocolate para niños | |
|---|---|---|
| **SPAGHETTI AND GARLIC BREAD**<br>**ESPAGHETI Y PAN DE AJO** | | **$2.99** |
| **DRUMSTICKS & FRIES**<br>**POLLO FRITO Y PAPITAS** | | **$2.99** |
| **CHEESE PIZZA with MEAT SAUCE**<br>**PIZZA DE QUESO con SALSA DE ESPAGHET** | | **$3.69** |
| **CHICKEN FINGERS with FRIES**<br>**PEDAZOS DE GALLINA FRITA con PAPITAS** | | **$3.69** |
| **BEER BATTER FISH FRY** (Wednesday & Friday only)<br>**PESCADO FRITO** (Miercoles Y Viernes solamente) | | **$2.99** |

tion, Salzer's staff is repeatedly drilled on how to treat "Robin's Pals" royally. To quote the training manual:

"As you may know, the kids of today are the customers of tomorrow. Kids will influence their parents on their decision of where to dine. We at Robin's understand this and go the extra yard to provide an upscale family atmosphere.

"Customers who are accompanied by children present a great opportunity for you to give that extra service. By being attentive, sympathetic, and helpful, you can greatly add to the convenience and enjoyment of their dining experience.

"Parents of young children will generally be happy to reward you with a good tip if it is obvious that the service you provide goes above and beyond the call of duty.

"Always remember that parents of small children never tire of hearing their children praised. It is always nice to compliment the children on their good behavior or manners. If the kids are not behaving well, compliment the parents on their child's cuteness."

Finally, under "Kids Procedures," it is noted that all kids receive:

1. a children's menu
2. a birthday club card
3. a toy or novelty
4. a balloon when leaving
5. a smile

## WORTH ROARRRING ABOUT

Families hunting for quality meals at value prices in the Bay area often wind up at Lyon's Restaurant. But rather than allow the dining room to be transformed into a jungle by mischievous little monkeys and other wild beasties, a children's menu to color was introduced by the 81-unit chain, headquartered in Foster City, California. (See Figure 3–12.)

**Lyons Children's Menu**
(For our friends 12 and under)

New! French Toast Fingers 'N Bacon or Sausage ....$1.95

Pancakes 'N Bacon or Sausage ...................$1.95

1 Egg 'N Bacon or Sausage...................$1.95

New! Pepperoni Pizza...$2.95

Fried Chicken Strips with French Fries.........$2.25

New! Fun Shapes Fish Sticks with French Fries.........$2.25

Hot Dog with French Fries.................$2.25

Hamburger with French Fries.................$2.25

New! Peanut Butter and Jelly with Fruit .....$1.95

Grilled Cheese with French Fries.................$1.95

**Drinks and Sweets**
Milk, Chocolate Milk, Lemonade, Soft Drinks .....75

Small Ice Cream or Pudding......................75

Child Size Shake or Sundae........................95

Figure 3-12    Coloring menu (courtesy of Lyon's, Foster City, CA)

The menu, which doubles as a placemat, comes in three different versions and features the operation's namesake, a lion, in various guises. Simple word games (unscramble the letters, fill in the blanks), mazes, tic-tac-toe boards, and dot-to-dot pictures are provided to tame the 10-and-under set until feeding time arrives. Upon being seated, each child also receives four crayons in a box printed with Lyon's logo.

Those whose stomachs are on empty may fill up on trusted hamburgers and hot dogs or dive into something different, such as fish-shaped fish sticks. There are also three breakfast items listed on the menu, including French Toast Fingers, all priced at $1.95.

## THE COLOR OF SUCCESS

Colors Cafe, a casual eatery in the beach community of Encinitas, California, is aptly named, according to manager Mary Bishop. Colorful posters hang from pale lavender walls, topped with a free-form, multicolored border. Goldenrod, hot pink, blueberry, teal, and grape splash servers' uniforms. The colors are repeated on tablecloths and 72-some upholstered chairs inside while outdoors, big, bright umbrellas shade additional seating for 38.

The menu is also a kaleidoscope of pizzas, pastas, salads and sandwiches, fresh seafood, and health food fare. (See Figure 3–13.) And it's color-coded. Green dots indicate that the item is a go for vegetarians. Yellow dots yield to meatless eaters on even stricter diets, who refrain from dairy foods as well. Blue dots are for kids.

"We attract a real mixture of people, including a lot of families with children," said Bishop. Of those customers 12 and younger, Bishop estimates that 80 percent of them order the specialty of the house: Kids' Gummy Bear Pizza ($3.95).

Don't take the listing literally. Soft, chewy, stick-to-the-teeth sweets are not applied on cheese and dough and baked in the oven. Rather, the signature item is prepared by cutting regular pizza dough with a cookie cutter into an eight-inch-high bear shape, which is topped with cheese, sliced black olives for eyes, a caper for a nose, and sliced red pepper for the mouth.

After the child has finished eating, and only after mom and/or dad gives the server permission, is the dessert—gummy bears—brought out.

On Halloween, the pizza bear is dressed in a costume. On Thanksgiving, he gets a pilgrim's hat. The breakfast menu, available on weekends, offers another variation. Gummy Bear Breakfast Pizza (also $3.95) is prepared with tomato sauce, scrambled eggs, potatoes, and bacon.

"Our Gummy Bear Pizza is a big hit that works well with parents too," said Bishop.

"Since families are important to us, the staff makes an effort to welcome children and treat them very special. Each child is given

## PIZZAS

*COLORS' PIZZAS ARE MADE WITH A 10" HOMEMADE CRUST
PREPARED WITH THE FRESHEST INGREDIENTS AND VEGETABLE OILS*

● MARGHARITA........$6.75
*The original pizza...marinara sauce, mozzarella and
fresh basil*

PEPPERONI.........$6.95
*Marinara sauce, pepperoni, mozzarella, Italian herbs
and seasoning*

● FOUR CHEESE.......$7.95
*Mozzarella, jalapeno jack, cheddar and goat cheese,
fresh basil, oregano and scallions*

GRILLED SHRIMP...$11.95
*Spicy Szechuan sauce, garlic, bean sprouts, sun dried
tomatoes, green onions, parsley, mozzarella and a
bountiful amount of grilled shrimp*

● PESTO.............$7.75
*Pesto sauce, chopped tomatoes, fresh basil and
walnuts*

COLORS HOT
ITALIAN SAUSAGE...$7.95
*Marinara and pesto sauce, Colors hot Italian sausage,
green pepper, black olives, onions, garlic,
mozzarella and oregano*

HAWAIIAN..........$7.95
*Marinara sauce, ham, fresh pineapple, almonds and
mozzarella*

SPINACH CAESAR
SALAD.............$7.75
*Fresh spinach, bacon, diced tomatoes, Caesar salad
dressing, garlic and parmesan cheese*
**With anchovies............................add $0.50**

● VEGETARIAN........$8.25
*Olive oil, Balsamic vinegar and fresh basil dressing,
with sliced tomatoes, artichoke hearts, mushrooms,
green peppers, spinach, onions, bean sprouts, black
olives, garlic, cumin and soy cheese*

JIMMY'S CHICKEN...$7.95
*Marinara sauce, chicken diced and marinated in fresh
herbs, tumaric and oriental chili garlic sauce,
topped with mozzarella and oregano*

● GOAT CHEESE.......$7.95
*Herbed olive oil, roasted garlic, chopped tomatoes,
green onions, fresh basil and goat cheese*

LONE STAR.........$7.75
*Homemade chili, red onions, jalapenos, cheddar cheese
and sour cream*

SOUTH OF THE
BORDER...........$8.25
*Homemade salsa, grilled chicken, sliced tomatoes,
onions, jalapenos and jack cheese*

THAI CHICKEN.....$8.50
*Spicy sate sauce, chicken, bean sprouts, water
chestnuts, red bell peppers, sesame seeds and
mozzarella*

JILL'S
HAM & SPINACH.....$7.95
*Olive oil, Balsamic vinegar and fresh basil dressing,
spinach leaves, diced tomatoes, ham, garlic and
mozzarella*

● KID'S GUMMY BEAR PIZZA .....$3.95
*Cheese and pepperoni pizza with a "colorful" side order of Gummy Bears*

● *VEGETARIAN ITEMS CONTAINING DAIRY PRODUCTS*

● *VEGETARIAN ITEMS CONTAINING NO DAIRY PRODUCTS*

● *SERVED ONLY TO OUR SPECIAL FRIENDS UNDER TWELVE AND OVER SIXTY*

*ALL ITEMS ON OUR MENU ARE AVAILABLE FOR TAKE-OUT*

Figure 3-13   Color-coded kids' menu (courtesy of Colors Cafe,
Encinitas, CA)

crayons and coloring sheets, which are usually on seasonal subjects. Then we hang their efforts on a 'wall of fame' for all to see," she added.

## FAIR SHARE PRICING STRUCTURE

The Peddler is in Gatlinburg, Tennessee, in the foothills of the Great Smoky Mountains, on the banks of the Little Pigeon River, in a log cabin that housed pioneers at the turn of the nineteenth century. This 165-seat restaurant, specializing in steak and prime rib, has been a destination for families celebrating special occasions or just passing through Great Smoky Mountains National Park since 1976.

"Families are the backbone of our business," said Rick Jones. According to the general manager, they come for the view, the high-quality food, the friendly service, and the value. A creative pricing strategy for children adds to the perception that money is being well spent.

The children's menu features four items available on the regular menu. (See Figure 3–14.) Portions are reduced, and the charge is just 50 cents multiplied by the child's age. With the maximum set at 12 years old, the most parents pay is $6.00 for prime rib, boneless chicken breast, charbroiled steak, or jumbo fried shrimp dinners, accompanied by a 40-item salad bar, french fries, bread, and a beverage. The salad bar only is just 35 cents times the child's age. Those under three eat for free.

All of this information is contained on a cleverly designed menu that resembles a greeting card. Open the cover, and a bear pops out.

"The die-cut design was an expense to create, manufacture, and print," said Jones. "But the favorable response has made it all worthwhile. Children also keep it as a souvenir, something to re-member us by in years to come."

Meanwhile, to keep children occupied and add to grown-ups' dining pleasure, The Peddler provides packets of four crayons and a proprietary coloring sheet. When entrees do arrive, servers are

Figure 3-14   Kid-priced menu (courtesy of The Peddler, Gatlinburg, TN)

trained to provide an extra nice touch. Jones said, "They ask to cut up the children's portions so adults can get right into eating theirs."

## ROOM SERVICE RINGS UP SALES

In a place where the air is laden with the sweet scent of chocolate, a popular destination for kids ages one to 100 is the 250-room Hotel Hershey in Hershey, Pennsylvania—home of America's most renowned chocolate manufacturer.

To accommodate more young guests' requests in the summer-

Figure 3-15   Kids' nighttime snack menu (courtesy of The Hotel
Hershey, Hershey, PA)

time, which is the busiest season, room service offers a special selection of kids' favorite snacks. The "at Night Fun Menu" is available daily from 9 P.M. to midnight from June through Labor Day. (See Figure 3–15.)

Included are five different potato dishes (ranging from plain fries at $1.95 to pizza fries topped with tomato sauce and cheese at $2.95 to "Simply Skins" with cheddar, bacon, and sour cream dip at $5.95), three variations of hot dogs, five types of cold sub sandwiches, and pizza.

"Our pricing structure for a 14-inch, family-size pizza is right in line with Pizza Hut's," said Ed Schopf, director of food and beverage. "We even offer it with a liter of Coke."

For those seeking sweeter treats, options include six cookies at $3.75. Add a carafe of milk, and the ante goes up to $6.50.

To stir up business during other times of the year, Hotel Hershey also sponsors theme weekends. "Kids Are Special" is a relatively new addition to the line-up, held over President's Day in February. Like the long-standing "Chocolate Lover's Weekend," kids' activities include everything from chocolate bingo to an "everybody's birthday party," complete with cake (chocolate, of course) and a make-your-own sundae bar.

# Chapter Four

# *Kids' Meals and Other Deals*

In the late 1970s an advertising executive working on a major fast food account came up with a concept that would permanently change children's perceptions of what a restaurant meal should be. The year was 1977. The chain was McDonald's. And the concept was "Happy Meals."

Suddenly, dining out—even in the most ordinary of settings—became a very special event. For Junior and Little Miss, what a treat to find their favorite foods, plus a toy or trinket, in a goodie box that doubled as a game and activity board. The chain passed on the cost of packaging and the premium to consenting adults, who considered the increased price a fair exchange for a little peace at lunch or dinner. Repeat business boomed. McDonald's prospered. Everybody was, as the name implied, happy.

In short order, multiunit quickservice competitors began following the leader, lighting up menu boards and the faces of children across the nation with variations on the boxed meal theme. Over time the game attracted new players, who bent the rules, developed alternate strategies, upped the ante, and offered even more fun fringe benefits—all in an effort to win a greater share of children's business.

## ADVANTAGES OF KIDS' MEALS

Today, kids' meals have not only saturated the fast food segment, but they are frequently tied into small chains' and independents' total marketing and promotional programs. The novelty may have worn off, but there are still valid reasons for keeping them around.

- Ordering is easy with kids' meals. In a convenience-driven society, parents appreciate a predetermined purchase decision.
- Kids' meals can't be shared. Hamburgers, hot dogs, french fries, and soft drinks can be split. But it is virtually impossible to cut a toy in half and expect to produce two smiles. Purchasing a separate meal for each child increases check averages. "When the sales of the transaction increase, operators profit. It's a profit that they wouldn't get otherwise without a kids' meal program in place," said Barry Busch, president of Admark, Inc., a leading supplier of kids' meal packaging materials and premium items in Topeka, Kansas.
- Kids' meals help eliminate the veto vote. Children wield tremendous influence in deciding where to dine. They're sophisticated, savvy, and not easily persuaded. Yet even the brightest tykes would have a hard time building a respectable case against an operation offering them a special meal with a neat toy treat.
- Kids' meals help build repeat business. By linking premiums to collectable series, children will want to return again and again to acquire entire sets.

## WHAT ABOUT PACKAGING? BAG IT!

The options in kids' meals containers range from houses, castles, and circus tents (with die-cut windows, doors, and flaps, complete with punch-out figures) to cardboard configurations of jungle beasts, farm-friendly animals, extinct and endangered species, classic cars, trains, tugboats, baseball mitts. The list goes on.

However, the shape of things to come just may be sacks. "The most significant trend in the last few years has been a shift from boxes to bags," said Admark's Busch.

Environmental concerns are, in part, responsible for the change. Public opinion favors cutting back waste. And paper is generally perceived to be easier to recycle than cardboard cartons. Cost is certainly another factor, with boxes priced up to three times higher than paper bags, according to Tom Symalla, president of Promotions, Inc. in St. Paul, Minnesota. The 17-year veteran of the foodservice business has found that those choosing to go with sacks and save may opt to discount kids' meals. Or they may elect to spend bigger bucks on giveaways.

"Most smaller operators on limited budgets are channeling packaging funds into premiums," Busch confirmed.

Which is exactly the case at Bob's Burger Express, headquartered in Salem, Oregon. In an independent study conducted by Marlene Wellin, the 14-unit chain's marketing and advertising director, young customers were asked what they preferred: the box that contained their meal or the toy inside.

"They liked the premium," said Wellin. Then, to confirm her findings, she surveyed the trash and found that, indeed, a fair share of packaging was winding up in the trash bins. "So I'm putting my money in toys."

## IT'S WHAT'S INSIDE THAT COUNTS

Kids like premiums, but not just any trinket will do.

"Kids are smart," said Busch. "They understand junk immediately."

According to Busch, toys that are a dime a dozen are a waste of money. It pays to seek out quality playthings and proprietary goods or to latch onto licensed products that are readily identifiable. More upfront money may be required, but the price of the premium may be passed down to the consumer in the cost of the packaged meal.

To shop for great buys, walk through restaurant shows and scour catalogs. Check the pulse of popular culture by watching current movies or tuning in to any children's television or radio network. Spend Saturday morning studying cartoons and commercials. Look at your customers. What are they wearing? What are they carrying?

## A PREMIUM PRIMER

Here are some additional tips on how to spot quality premiums that will push kids' hot buttons, are right on the money, and are right for the times.

- Look for items that require some hands-on fun, items that kids are able to put together and put to use.
- Don't ignore tried-and-true favorites. Wellin of Bob's Burger Express said, "We recently gave away an old-fashioned jar of bubbles with all kids' meals. They went crazy! And parents perceived it as a very good value because the container was a nice size."
- Items with educational merit are highly prized by parents.
- Try to find unisex items. Generally, Wellin has found that boys won't touch "girl things" like dolls, especially those that begin with the letter "B." However, girls are more receptive to typical boy toys (cars, sports paraphernalia). "We featured kids' meals in boxes shaped like baseball gloves," said Wellin. "I put a baseball card in each box, and all kids loved the promotion."

Symalla of Promotions, Inc. suggests that if a boy-oriented premium is offered during one promotional period, something special for girls or with widespread appeal should be featured the next time.

- Look for items that will build repeat business and satisfy kids seeking variety in life. Collectable toys (such as a series of small figures from the same cartoon, troll dolls, glasses, sports cars, etc.) are always well received.

- Changing premiums every two to three months is an incentive to bring back business.

- Buying in quantities usually saves money. But if you don't have the storage space, find out beforehand if unsold merchandise is returnable. Base purchase decisions on how many kids' meals you've sold in the past, and how many you expect to sell in the near future. The key is to make sure supply meets demand. Nothing destroys momentum more than running out of premiums before the promotion has run its course.

- Make sure the item is kid-safe, especially for little children. If there are small parts, have an alternate selection for infants and toddlers, who love to put everything—especially things that don't belong there—in their mouths.

## GREAT GIVEAWAYS

Kids are fickle. What's awesome today may be a total turnoff tomorrow. There are no guarantees what will please. Still, experts in the field of premiums and packaging maintain that the following items are clearly winners:

- Trolls, those good luck dolls with wild hair in a rainbow of colors, appear to have broken the sex/gender barrier
- Three-D glasses, accompanied by comic, coloring, or activity books
- Reuseable, removeable stickers
- Friendship bracelets and plastic wrist bands
- Neon shoelaces
- Sidewalk chalk
- Water bottles
- Reuseable "magic doodle" notepads

- Pull-back sports cars
- Dinosaurs

## FOODS TO GO

There is one more crucial element in a kids' meal: the meal itself. Kids never seem to tire of a hamburger or cheeseburger, fries, and a small beverage (milk, juice, a soft drink, or a shake). Other foods that travel well and help broaden menu appeal include:

- Chicken fingers or nuggets
- Chicken wings or drumsticks
- Hot dogs
- Pizza
- Grilled cheese sandwiches
- Breakfast sandwiches (such as English muffin pizzas topped with tomato sauce, scrambled eggs, and cheese)
- Submarine sandwiches
- Baked stuffed potatoes
- Ribs
- Mini-tacos
- Quesadillas stuffed with plain cheese or cheese and crumbled bacon bits
- Egg rolls
- Carrot and celery sticks
- Fresh fruit cups
- Fruit and vegetable kebabs
- Muffins and milk

## A WORD OF ADVICE

They may be listed as "kids' meals" on menus and menuboards. But don't overlook the fact that the underlying purpose of packaging special meals for children is to appease grown-ups. When children are placated and entertained, parent satisfaction is guaranteed.

As the following case studies prove, the most effective kids' meals are those particularly suited to an operation's overall marketing strategy.

## SUB OPERATOR SUBSCRIBES TO KIDS' MEALS

When Jerry Borton first came aboard Port of Subs as director of marketing, kids' meals consisted of a three-inch sandwich, small chips, and a small drink packed in a generic cardboard container. It was time for Port of Subs to take a more aggressive stance and establish a greater presence in the family market. The "me generation" was turning into the "us age." And the Port of Subs product line—freshly prepared hot and cold submarine sandwiches, salads, and soups—couldn't be more in line with baby boomers' demands for fresh, healthy alternatives to burgers and fried foods.

In charting a course directed toward kids, the 70-unit chain, stationed in Reno, Nevada, began by creating theme characters: the Captain of Quality, with sidekicks Subby (a boat) and Sammy (a seahorse).

The captain, a friendly guy sporting shades and an oversized mustache, is described by Borton as "a cool dude in a loose mood." He is featured on the customized meal cartons, which are die-cut into ship shapes. Kids still get a three-inch sandwich (the most popular being turkey, plain, hold the lettuce and tomatoes), chips, and a beverage. But there's more in store inside, including an eight-page coloring book featuring the captain and crew and an aquatic toy, such as a dolphin, pelican, whale, or shark. (See Figure 4–1.)

"Kids like to play. Adults like something more educational. We're trying to provide the highest mix," said Borton.

"When we first instituted the program, we changed the coloring book and premiums once a month to prevent children from getting bored. Now we coordinate kids' premiums into our corporate promotional campaigns, and change them about seven times a year," he added.

## Sammy the Seahorse.

Figure 4-1    Theme characters coloring book (courtesy of Port of Subs, Reno, NV)

Since launching the program, consumption of kids' meals has increased from 35 percent to 50 percent, according to Borton. "When we started, about 130 kids' meals were sold per store per month. Now we're doing just under 200. It's hard to know exactly how much they've contributed to Port of Subs' overall sales because kids don't come alone. They bring in their parents. But our figures show that, chainwide, sales are up 12 percent this year," he said.

"We think that it's been important to have proprietary items, to have specific things that no one else has."

Also helping to keep Port of Subs' name in the public eye are the Captain of Quality's frequent guest appearances at grand openings, rodeos, parades, and other community events. "Someone gets in a costume and actually plays him," explained Borton. As the story goes, the crusty captain has lost his voice at sea and can't speak. So he is always attended by a first mate who helps him hand out

Sammy is on his way to Port of Subs
to get dinner for his family.

balloons and premium items, and does the talking for him. That way, children aren't confused even if a woman is featured in the starring role.

A commitment to promoting children's business as a total experience has also led to Port of Subs-sponsored field trips. Franchised units are encouraged to contact local elementary schools, and invite kindergartners through third-graders to tour their facilities on Monday through Thursday mornings, prior to opening.

The program begins with a history of Port of Subs followed by an explanation of the four food groups. After pointing out that grains, dairy products, meats, and vegetables make up almost all Port of Subs' sandwiches, a back-of-house tour commences. Teachers demonstrate how to prepare sandwiches, and all students receive free kids' meals. Each visitor also receives an activity sheet that contains three different money-saving coupons. (See Figure 4–2.)

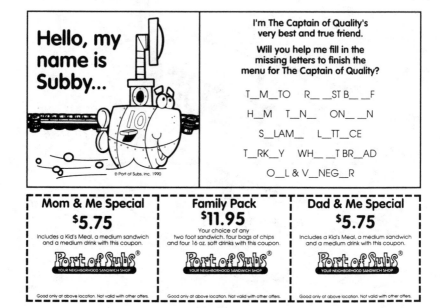

Figure 4-2    Field trip activity sheet (courtesy of Port of Subs, Reno, NV)

One is for a special deal on a "Family Pack" (a two-foot sandwich, four bags of chips, and four soft drinks for $11.95). The other coupons acknowledge new family dynamics and offer "Dad and Me" and "Mom and Me" discounts (a kids' meal, a medium sandwich, and a medium drink for $5.75).

## KIDS' MEALS TAKE OFF

With an increase in single-parent households, airlines have seen the rise of a new class of frequent flyer—kids shuttling back and forth between divorced mom and dad. Recognizing the long-term potential of this small but growing and extremely influential market, Delta Air Lines pioneered what it touts as "the most comprehensive kids' marketing program available today." The Fantastic Flyer program includes a kids' club designed to instill a feeling of belonging in all members, and a quarterly magazine with a circulation of 1.1 million readers from around the world.

There is also the program's Disney-designed mascot, "an intelligent and charming" cartoon character who goes by the name of Dusty the Delta Air Lion, according to Margaret Ross, coordinator of marketing communications. And there are Dusty's Dens, which are welcome retreats for weary little travelers making connections in hub airports. These special rooms for supervised play are stocked with games, toys, and movies.

Special kids' meals have only recently been added to the Fantastic Flyer program. However, recipients will find the wait well worth it, according to Ross.

First, kids' meals are delivered in "Caboodles"—colorful, plastic, reuseable containers resembling small tackle boxes with handles.

"The fact that children like to carry containers gave us the idea of how to package their meals," Ross said.

Inside the Caboodles are activity sheets with dot-to-dot, fill-in-the-blank, and other assorted games, plus four to six different playthings, ranging from Barbie Doll cars to NFL trading cards.

"We're continually changing and updating the offerings so our frequent flyers aren't bored," said Ross. "Children get to take the toy kits home with them. So everyone has a little gift when they deplane."

As for the meal itself, Delta did extensive research before deciding to go with the safest bets, the foods with the most widespread appeal. Breakfast includes cereal, juice, a banana, and a muffin. Lunch and dinner options include pepperoni pizza or chicken nuggets, served with curly fries, juice and milk, grapes, and gummy bears.

The Atlanta, Georgia-based airline requires six hours' notice to order (standard procedure for all special meal requests).

While it may be too early to tell whether Delta's investment will pay off in the future, the carrier believes that it's on the right track.

"Marketing to children is a smart thing to do," said Ross. "It's a long-term commitment. We're waiting for them to grow up."

## FUN IS THE NAME OF THE GAME

When Bill Long, brand marketing director of Wendy's International, inherited the Dublin, Ohio, hamburger chain's kids' program recently, he was ready to put it to sleep. After all, Wendy's had positioned itself as an adult-oriented restaurant unlike its major competitor, McDonald's, where the entire atmosphere is geared toward kids. Why risk upsetting a loyal adult customer base?

Looking at the research, he decided to proceed.

"The key is kids' drive-in business because they bring in a lot of drag-along sales," said Long. Plus, he didn't want Wendy's to lose out on the veto vote. To attract families, you've got to get their children's approval. "And what really draws kids is fun," he added.

With kids' meals back on the agenda, Long took another look at research.

"We found out that kids don't like to carry boxes in hand outside of the restaurant," he said. "So we went to bags that are interactive. We also found that food is subordinate to fun. The premium is very important.

"As a result, you have to come up with something fun, something different every six to eight weeks."

In describing how that feat is accomplished, Long said, "You work with the small universe of people who deal in premiums, most of whom have come over from toy manufacturers. And you test a year out in advance."

Wendy's identifies its kid customers as being a little older than those frequenting McDonalds—in the five- to 10-year-old range. As a result, they demand items that are more sophisticated than figurines.

"They do know junk," added Long. "They'll buy it one time, then they won't come back. And they do have very long memories."

"A lot of people go with licensing," he said. "But on a 50 cent premium, five to 10 percent of the cost goes toward royalties. If it's a success, you're going to run out. If it's unsuccessful, you have all these things left over. So why not take the money you'd pay in royalties, and put it back into engineering and design?

Figure 4-3   Kids' menu (courtesy of Mels Drive-In, San Francisco, CA)

"Over the past few years, we haven't paid for any licensing and have had one successful premium on top of another."

Long credits "speed writers"—five-inch, classic-looking pull-back cars that transform into pens—for putting Wendy's on the kids' meal map. He came up with the idea for the novel premium while shopping in toy stores in Tokyo, Japan. Back in the United States, Long also scouts the gift industry for inspiration.

"We're not in the children's business," stressed Long. "But

families are important to us. We get parents by reinforcing a quality menu, variety, and value. And we get the kids to say okay to Wendy's by reinforcing fun."

## KIDS' MEALS BUILD TABLESERVICE RESTAURANT BUSINESS, TOO

Kids love to eat at Mels Drive-in in San Francisco, California. The fact of the matter is, Mels loves kids for the business they drive in.

"Children account for 25 percent of our customers. You can walk in the restaurant at any time of day, and find them. We have a corner on the market here," said Gabriel Mendez, general manager.

The kid biz grew naturally, starting back in the mid-1980s when the diner first opened.

"When we realized that we were attracting a lot of children, we decided to cater to them," Mendez said. "We came up with a menu and special kids' meals served in boxes shaped like 1950s-style cars. They fit in with the theme." (See Figure 4–3.)

The combo meals range from a burger and fries ($4.45) to fish and chips ($4.45) to fried chicken and fries ($5.75), and include a choice of beverage.

In addition to the cardboard cars, which they get to take home, children also receive free balloons and, according to Mendez, free rein "to run around the restaurant and go crazy."

# Chapter Five

# *Packaging Promotions for Fun and Profits*

In today's highly competitive market, fun promotions appealing to children and parents have become serious business.

- It's holiday time! Come in for a special meal!
- It's your birthday! Join the club!
- It's Sunday night! Eat for free!
- An all-A student! Dinner's on the house!
- Come tour the kitchen! Return with the family for a discounted meal!
- What a beautiful picture! Be sure and enter the coloring contest!
- Bring teddy bear to brunch!
- Enjoy breakfast with Santa!
- Meet Mickey and Minnie for lunch!

Whatever the offer, be it a once-a-year extravaganza or an ongoing campaign, a big budget production or a small-scale event, the motivating factors remain the same. Promotions are staged to break the monotony, add value, lure new customers, establish loyalties with repeat clientele, and ring up additional sales.

Families are particularly receptive to meal deals. As NPD CREST research has found, "Families with kids have a much greater propensity to take advantage of deals when they go out to eat than does the public at large. Their propensity to use deals is nearly 40 percent above that noted for all households."

Twofer ones, freebies, dollars-off coupons, dining with cartoon characters—parents and children aren't choosy. They like all promotions. Reports NPD CREST, "In looking at the types of deals that are used by parties with kids, we find that they are somewhat more inclined to use coupons than the general public. They also take advantage of other deal offers. This likely reflects the group's propensity to take advantage of specially priced kids' menus and other promotions directed towards children . . . glasses, toys, games, etc."

## LIMITED FUNDS ARE NO LIMIT TO FUN

When it comes to staging promotions, what counts even more than money are good ideas. Fortunately, creative concepts are within every operator's means.

- Many of the best business boosters featured in this chapter grew out of brainstorming sessions. Get together with experienced associates. Or plan an informal gathering of managers and waitstaff who are on the front lines every day, meeting and greeting customers. They may have priceless insight to share about the character and needs of the families frequenting your operation.

- Sponsor an employee incentive program centered around an in-house competition for the best publicity stunt, game, gimmick, or promotional program. Reward the creator of the most original concept with a monetary bonus or time off for good behavior.

- From little minds come BIG ideas. Invite children of staff or children of regular customers to a focus group. Foot the bill for the participants' favorite meals. Then steer the discussion to the topic of how to put more fun into the dining experience.

- Identify your audience and set objectives. These are elementary principles of promotion planning, but are particularly critical when children are the target market.

"You've got to hit their hot buttons," said Ron Berryman, who heads Berryman Communications Co., a kids' consumer promotion agency in Chicago, Illinois. "If the promotion is too broad-based, it doesn't work." Preschoolers are quite different than five- to seven-year-olds, according to Berryman. After that, kids change in two-year increments (eight to 10, 11 to 13, etc.), always seeking to emulate the group preceding them. "When developing promotions, keep age groups in mind," he said.

Remember, too, that one gem of an idea may be enough to generate sales and get traffic rolling. But to keep business momentum building, think long-term (i.e., multigenerational, cradle to grave). An ongoing program of children's promotions should be incorporated into a larger marketing plan designed to encompass something for everyone.

## THE abC'S OF KIDS' PROMOTIONS

In general, children's promotions fall into categories, which we'll call the "Five C's":

- Clubs
- Contests
- Cash Discounts
- Co-op Programs
- Class Acts

## KIDS' CLUBS

In January 1990 the second largest burger chain in the world made news by launching a direct attack on its number one competitor. Burger King's ammunition, designed to loosen McDonald's foothold on the children's market, was a brand-new "Kids' Klub."

Response was overwhelming. More than 500,000 founding members signed on in the first quarter. Backed by the support of national advertising, an aggressive direct mail campaign, and professionally polished collateral material, membership zoomed to 3.8 million by June 1992, with an estimated 95,000 applications pouring in each month. The "Kids' Club Meal" became the Miami, Florida-based chain's fastest growing entree.

McDonald's still reigns tops with kids. But Burger King has gained ground in the family trade and has amassed a share of this sizable market.

The lesson to be learned from the BK experience? A kids' club may not dethrone the competition. But when added to your marketing arsenal, it proves a pretty powerful aid in improving family relations and increasing kids' market share.

Granted, the vast majority of operators lack the resources and wherewithal to create kids' clubs on the magnitude of a major chain's. This needn't be a deterrent; there are plenty of programs to start on a shoestring.

Birthday clubs seem to be the most cost-effective and popular formats nationwide. To join, children ages 10 to 12 and younger are usually required to fill out a form, stating their name, address, and date of birth. After turning in their vital statistics, they may simply be instructed to return on their birthdays with their families to enjoy one free kids' meal or a free dessert (such as brownie a la mode, cupcake, slice of cake, or hot fudge sundae topped with sprinkles and an ignited sparkler). Or the information may be put into a computer. As the big day approaches, cards addressed to birthday boys and girls, along with invitations to come back for the free food offer, are then sent through the mail.

Since starting its birthday club, Mitzel's American Kitchen in Seattle, Washington, has enrolled 20,000 members.

"Each child receives a postcard inviting them in for a free kids' meal during their birthday. We've seen a 33 percent redemption rate company-wide with this promotion," said Katherine Jacobsen, marketing manager.

Inexpensive to implement, relatively easy to execute, and a way to motivate repeat business, it's no wonder so many choose this straightforward approach.

A frequent diners' club program is another feasible format with widespread appeal. Membership's main privilege is a card, which is stamped or punched each time the diner visits the establishment. After a specified number of visits has been recorded, the card may be redeemed for merchandise or meals.

Whatever the details of the deal, the rules and regulations, all kids' clubs offer these advantages:

- They build goodwill among families, who are more promotion-oriented than the public at large.
- They build repeat business, not only with kids but with the families and friends who always accompany them.
- Responses may be tracked to analyze the promotion's profitability and its impact on sales and traffic.
- They help develop a direct mail base of proven customers, who may be targeted with newsletters, valued customer coupon programs, or announcements of upcoming special events at the operation.
- They establish loyalties.

## KIDS' CONTESTS

Similar benefits are to be gained by giving children the opportunity to compete. Coloring contests, becoming increasingly prevalent industry-wide, have the added advantage of keeping active kids occupied from the time they are seated until their meals are served.

The rules of the game vary only slightly from operation to operation.

1. Each contestant receives crayons and a coloring sheet. (To be fair, players color the same picture. At Mitzel's, the picture appears on the back of the kids' menu.)

2. Have them sign each sheet with their name and address. (This will help you contact winners and build a mailing list.)

3. Instruct them to turn in the completed work to the server, cashier, host, or hostess.

4. There is no limit to the number of times each player may enter. (This builds repeat business.)

5. Winners are announced by mail, and awarded with a free kids' meal (another ploy to entice customers to come back). If funds allow, the entry goes into a bigger drawing for a higher-ticket item (such as a bicycle).

6. Winning pictures are displayed in a high-traffic area (providing more motivation to return to the establishment).

7. A new coloring contest begins each week, or a different coloring sheet is featured each month (again, to encourage repeat business).

Variation: Instead of a coloring sheet, contestants are given a blank piece of paper, and instructed to create their own drawing. Keep the subject simple and make sure that it's something universally recognizable (an item from the menu, such as a hot dog, or an image tied to the seasons, such as Santa Claus).

Note: If the entry form also serves as the child's placemat, caution the waitstaff to be very careful where they place food and beverages. Serious artists become very upset when their work is destroyed by the rings of a wet glass or by catsup or spaghetti sauce stains.

On what basis are entries judged? Operators admit off the record that they base their decisions on the quality of the work as well as the cuteness of the kid. Or they deem every child a winner, thereby increasing the chances that more young customers will return to redeem their free meals—bringing along assorted family members, who will have to pay for theirs.

## CASH DISCOUNTS

Children's meals are regularly priced as loss leaders. The rationale is that the lower the ticket items, the greater the perceived value. More traffic will result.

Grown-ups do find low prices a terrific inducement to come to a restaurant with their families. However, children are lured more by fun. Put the two together—good value plus great fun—and you've got yourself a profit-winning strategy.

The Ground Round accomplishes this feat with its "Just a Penny a Pound" pitch. Kids have a blast getting on a scale to find out how much they weigh, and adults delight in the bargain. (With the average child weighing 61 pounds, kids' meals cost just 61 cents on the nights when the promotion is offered.)

Another example of how to appeal to two different audiences simultaneously is "Little Muchachos Day," celebrated at Chi-Chi's in Woodbridge, New Jersey. To generate more family traffic on Sunday, the prices of all kids' meals are slashed in half. It's a bonus for grown-ups. What's more, a clown appears to entertain with face painting, washable tattoo artistry, and tricks. It's a kick for kids.

The moral of these stories, as well as those found on the upcoming pages, is obvious. The offer of money-saving meals earns the most profitable returns when packaged with interactive play for kids.

Here are some more creative methods of attracting children of all ages:

- Hold a story-and-snack hour for kids between breakfast and lunch or lunch and dinner. Charge a nominal fee (such as

$1.99 per child, $2.99 per adult) for a muffin and milk in mid-morning or a cup of soup and mini-sandwich (on a small dinner roll) in the late afternoon. Employ one of your staff, who is particularly good with children, to read a picture storybook borrowed from the public library. Announce the event on flyers, posted in the window of the operation and given out at the register. For virtually no money down, you'll be building traffic during traditionally slow periods, establishing a higher profile in the community, and, hopefully, expanding your customer base.

- Put teddy bears on parade. Offer a free or discounted kids' meal to any child who brings in a favorite stuffed toy. Or, given the popularity of trolls today, consider staging a troll bowl. The same offer applies to any child accompanied by a treasured troll doll. If possible, dress the host or hostess and servers in costumes appropriate to the theme to turn the dining area into an entertaining stage. And let them lead the parade of children and their dolls in a march around the restaurant.

- Candy Leonard of Familywise Associates, a consulting firm in Somersworth, New Hampshire, attests to the benefits of a working parents' dinner (in contrast to a businessmen's lunch or an early bird special for seniors). Set aside one slow night a week (Monday or Tuesday), and offer reduced prices on meals served family-style. Rent a VCR and tapes, and set up a section just for kids to screen PG movies or cartoons.

- To draw older children, invite them on behind-the-scenes tours conducted Saturday mornings or Sunday afternoons. For an all-inclusive low price, they also get to eat in the kitchen.

- Stage special tastings. Once a month, introduce a new item on the kids' menu. Offer it for free, and let young customers vote on whether to include it as a regular feature. Make up simple "thumbs up or thumbs down" ballots (that don't require reading), and instruct the electorate to drop off their votes in the ballot box positioned near the cash register.

## CO-OP PROGRAMS

"Restaurants have great tie-in opportunities with suppliers," said Ron Berryman of Berryman Communications. By establishing partnerships and pooling resources, both parties benefit. "And that's how you get really effective promotions."

Jon Ostrov, vice president of marketing of Carlson Companies' Country Kitchen, a 250-unit chain based in Minneapolis, Minnesota, drives home the point of how a co-op investment made it possible for a midsize family restaurant on a tight budget to compete in the promotional arena with the major chains.

As he recalled, a chance encounter with a juice manufacturer at a trade show dinner eventually developed into a mutually beneficial relationship.

"We got to talking about the popularity of juice boxes, and came up with the idea of serving his product in juice box protectors, embossed with both our logos," said Ostrov.

The protectors, in proprietary day-glo colors, went on sale in the restaurants in the spring. For $1.99, customers also received a juice box and a sheet of stickers featuring Calico Bear, Country Kitchen's mascot.

"Since the protectors retail for $1.99, customers actually got the juice and the stickers for free. Plus, they couldn't get those colors anywhere else," said Ostrov. "So that's an example where you take a good brand, that mothers trust, and give customers something that nobody else is doing, something really different."

## CLASS ACTS

Manufacturers and suppliers are one source to side with when creating promotions. Schools are another. For those in the foodservice industry seeking to make a real difference, the educational community provides unlimited opportunities for tie-in ventures.

There are basically two ways to get involved. Either the classroom comes to your door lured by field trips (enabling students to experience firsthand the day-to-day routines of a restaurant) or academic achievement incentives (such as treating outstanding students to free meals). Or you go into the schools and get involved in the curriculum.

The first step is to contact the local school administration to find out what, if any, programs exist and then offer your assistance.

- Target one school or a specific grade, and arrange to meet with teachers and staff.
- Find out where support is needed most.
- Work closely with educators to develop a program of instruction that is easy to use.
- If the program is to stand on its own, make it self-explanatory and self-contained so it can be easily adapted to any classroom setting.
- Don't be self-serving. Teachers and students alike will be automatically turned off by operators who put their interests ahead of educational objectives.
- Give the program a strong instructional base to make it appealing to teachers. At the same time, try to make it fun for students to learn.

Your efforts will earn high grades in the community. A positive public relations campaign is often rewarded with free media exposure. Plus, schools provide an outstanding and receptive network of potential customers, including children, teachers, staff, friends, and families.

## GO FOR THE GOLD

If there is one common attribute shared by all of the promotions featured in the upcoming pages it is this: they are winners. They help generate sales. They contribute to escalating traffic. They help increase repeat business. They build awareness in the community. They help establish high-profile images.

And if there is a lesson to be learned from the efforts of others it is that aggressive action pays off. Be smart. Rather than waiting for families with children to come to your door, go to them.

The following ideas should help you start formulating plans.

## BURGER CLUB

Eat at Ed's. Get a token. The more return trips you make, the more tokens you receive. The more tokens you have, the better free gifts you get.

That's basically the gist of Ed Debevic's "Burger Club," which is available at two out of the six 1950s-style diners in the Chicago, Illinois-based chain.

According to Ed's president, Gerard Centioli, the idea for the token redemption program came out of a brainstorming session. "One of the things that we pride ourselves on is creating concepts that meet the demands of the market. It was clear that when Lettuce Entertain You Enterprises formed Ed's in 1984, families were looking to enhance their dining experiences by taking the next step beyond fast food," said Centioli. "We were discussing how kids needed special attention, and the special ways that they could be served."

The resulting offer is now limited to locations in Deerfield, Illinois (a suburb of the Windy City), and Phoenix, Arizona— where kids make up a greater percentage of total customers than in the Chicago, New York, Beverly Hills, or Osaka, Japan locations.

A poker-like chip embossed in gold with "Ed Debevic's Short Order Deluxe" comes with every kids' meal. As explained on placemats, "If you're 12 or younger, when you order any Eddie Jr. meal, you'll get a Burger Club token free! You can collect and redeem them at Ed's Souvenir Stand for neat stuff. (Or, you can just throw them out. Your choice.)"

This latter option gets few takers, considering that even those seeking immediate gratification may redeem one token for mer-

Figure 5-1    Items that can be purchased with Burger Club
tokens from Ed's Burger Club (courtesy of Ed's, Deerfield, IL)

chandise ranging from a balloon imprinted with "Wise Up. Eat at Ed's." to an official Ed Debevic's paper soda jerk's hat to a small button that announces, "Eat and Get Out!" (See Figure 5–1.)

Understandably, the value of the prizes rises with the number of tokens in a child's possession.

"We get a lot of kids returning on a regular basis," said Centioli. "We try to make it nice for them to come back."

Rotating stock is another means of scoring points with regulars. Of the ever-changing selection of kazoos, sunglasses, buttons, and yo-yos, T-shirts, at six tokens each, are consistently the most popular.

"We do a lot of kids' parties, and one trend I've noticed is that kids will pool together their tokens to get a T-shirt to give to the birthday boy or girl. They really like them," said Centioli.

The other trend that Centioli spots has to do with food. Currently, the "Little Eddie" section of the menu features all the classic kids' favorites, served with fries, small drink, and a treat for $3.50. (The treat stands for the world's smallest hot fudge sundae and a chocolate chip cookie.)

"With increased interest in health, we're moving away from soft drinks and providing more fruit juice options," said Centioli. There is also talk of replacing the chocolate chip cookie with an OAT-MEAL chocolate chip.

## ADVENTURES OF THE BIG BOY

Children of the 1950s now bring their small fry to Big Boy, a pioneer in the field of family fun dining. For nearly four decades, guests 10 years old and younger have been greeted with "Adventures of the Big Boy," a comic book produced exclusively for the family restaurant chain. (See Figure 5–2.) In addition to featuring a different comic caper each month, the 16-page publication includes an application form to the oldest kids' club in existence in the American foodservice industry, plus letters to the restaurant's massive mascot, coloring and activity pages, a listing of potential pen

Figure 5-2   "Adventures of the Big Boy" comic book (courtesy of Big Boy/Elias Brothers Restaurants, Inc., Warren, MI)

pals, and a joke page. (See Figure 5–3.) The back cover is reserved for the children's menu.

"It [the comic book] was the first real tool in the restaurant industry to satisfy children," said Anthony Michaels, vice president of marketing of parent company Elias Brothers Restaurants, Inc. in Warren, Michigan. "It has definitely been a successful marketing device."

The comic book's creator and long-standing publisher, Manfred Bernhard, president of Webs Advertising Corp., Old Lyme, Connecticut, recounts that the original intent of the Adventure series was to keep kids so busy they wouldn't be able to disturb those patrons who weren't parents.

"We printed about 100,000 copies of the first issue, which was then distributed to less than 100 restaurants. Now there are close to 1,000 restaurants, and we print between 800,000 to 1,000,000 copies," said Bernhard.

The National Big Boy Club began a few months after the first issue appeared. Joining is (and has always been) free. (Individual restaurants pick up the tab.) Incentives for becoming a member include free burgers on birthdays and Christmas, a certificate, and a "secret decoder key" enabling those in the know to decipher the secret messages that appear throughout the comic books.

"We receive approximately 5,000 pieces of mail a month," said Bernhard. "When children write to us, they always get an answer. We keep communication constant between them and Big Boy, his friend Dolly, and his dog Nugget.

"We've also had many, many letters from parents saying that they were members of the Big Boy Club and are now signing up their kids," he added.

How does Bernhard account for the continuing success of the club and the timeless appeal of a comic book character, who still sports a 1950s-style ducktail hairdo and dresses in red-and-white checked overalls over a white T-shirt bearing his name?

"It [the club] makes children feel that they really belong, that they're part of a family," he said. "He [Big Boy] is just a nice kid who always tries to do the right thing, but it doesn't always work out in his favor. They can relate."

Figure 5-3   Big Boy comic book page (courtesy of Big Boy/Elias Brothers Restaurants, Inc., Warren, MI)

## CALLIN' ALL LIL' COWPOKES AND
## LIL' RANCH HANDS

"I never thought I'd see the day when we'd have changing tables in the women's rest rooms," said Michael Abbate, director of operations of A La Carte Entertainment Inc., Mt. Prospect, Illinois.

Throughout the 1970s and 1980s fern bars had been the specialty and singles the target market of the Chicago-area, multiconcept restaurant and nightclub operator. "But as our customers aged, we changed with the times," Abbate said. The greenery came down at two former swinging hot spots in the suburbs, country-western regalia was shipped in, and a new era of catering to families with children began with the opening of Dumas Walter's and Cadillac Ranch.

From Day One at the two restaurants, Abbate knew that he wanted to do more than offer crayons and coloring options to kids. So he tapped into the club concept.

To join the Lil' Cowpokes Club at Dumas Walter's or the Lil' Ranch Hands Club at Cadillac Ranch, all "youngins" are instructed to fill out an application form with their name, address, phone number, and birthdate, and "give it to one of our server folk." (See Figure 5–4.) In return, they receive a VIP card. On subsequent visits, whenever the card is shown, members are treated to a free brownie sundae.

Abbate's dividend from the kids' clubs is a mailing list of over 2,000-plus proven customers, which he uses to cross-market promotions.

"I never realized how many kids go out to eat with parents," he said. "You would not believe what it's done for business."

On Sunday only, between the hours of 3 and 9 P.M., the card admits all members into a game room, located in a small bar area at Dumas Walter's and in a separate banquet room at Cadillac Ranch. The children get straw cowboy hats to keep (at a cost to Abbate of $1.50 apiece) and free use of the carnival-type games, which are overseen by two former preschool teachers. In addition to playing bean toss, shooting baskets, and lassooing a life-size horse head,

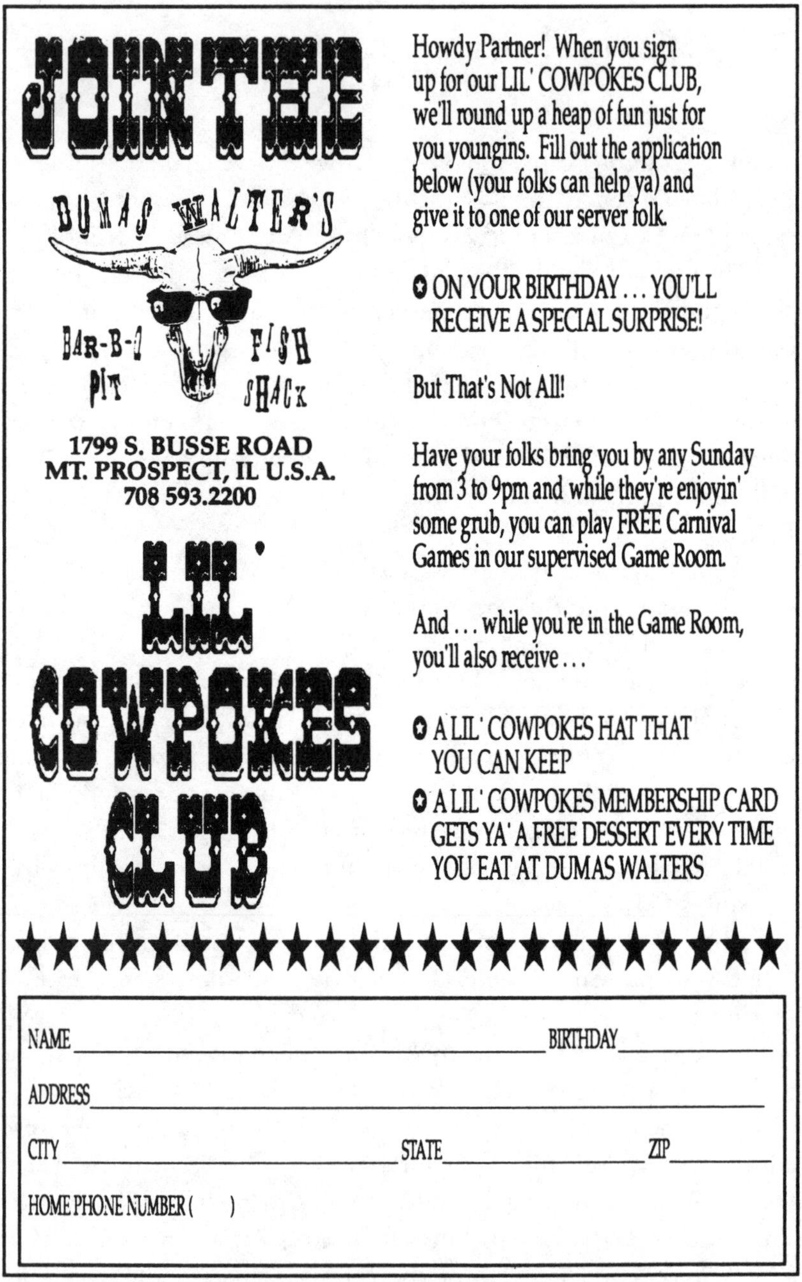

JOIN THE

DUMAS WALTER'S

BAR-B-1 PIT FISH SHACK

**1799 S. BUSSE ROAD
MT. PROSPECT, IL U.S.A.
708 593.2200**

LIL' COWPOKES CLUB

Howdy Partner! When you sign up for our LIL' COWPOKES CLUB, we'll round up a heap of fun just for you youngins. Fill out the application below (your folks can help ya) and give it to one of our server folk.

○ ON YOUR BIRTHDAY... YOU'LL RECEIVE A SPECIAL SURPRISE!

But That's Not All!

Have your folks bring you by any Sunday from 3 to 9pm and while they're enjoyin' some grub, you can play FREE Carnival Games in our supervised Game Room.

And... while you're in the Game Room, you'll also receive...

○ A LIL' COWPOKES HAT THAT YOU CAN KEEP
○ A LIL' COWPOKES MEMBERSHIP CARD GETS YA' A FREE DESSERT EVERY TIME YOU EAT AT DUMAS WALTERS

★★★★★★★★★★★★★★★★★★★★★★★★★★★

NAME _____ BIRTHDAY _____

ADDRESS _____

CITY _____ STATE _____ ZIP _____

HOME PHONE NUMBER ( )

Figure 5-4 Kids' club application from Dumas Walter's (courtesy of A La Carte Entertainment Inc., Mt. Prospect, IL)

face-painting, arts and crafts projects, and sing-along cartoon videos keep the very young very happy.

Every Sunday during the fall, Cadillac Ranch also offers free hay rides.

"It costs us $400 per day for the Clydesdale horse-drawn cart, but it's worth it," said Abbate. "Dinner business has never been better. We get waits of up to one hour."

Now, given such a success rate, it may be only a matter of time until changing tables are added to the men's rooms as well.

## COLOR A WINNER

"We realized a long time ago that children are the ones who decide where to eat. When we do get them in the restaurant, our main marketing objective is to treat them like gods," said John Berres, owner of Cafe Flavors in Charlotte, North Carolina.

So they'll be sure and return with families and friends in tow, the casual eatery sponsors an ongoing coloring contest for all 12-and-under patrons.

The cover of the children's menu features a black-and-white rendering of the pair of lips that is Cafe Flavors' logo. Pint-sized participants are instructed by managers to color in the lip-smacking picture as creatively as possible, write their name and address on the contest entry form (see Figure 5–5), and submit it to the front desk for judging. Two winners, awarded the grand prize of one free dinner each, are announced weekly. The best artistic expressions are put on display in the front of the restaurant.

"Since we probably give away more kids' meals than we sell, we're not actually making money on them," said Berres. "But we're building repeat business with parents, whom we see coming back on their own."

Stern's, a 22-unit chain of department stores headquartered in Paramus, New Jersey, lures young starving artists by running a similar coloring contest in all six of its public restaurants. As soon as children 11 and under are seated, they receive a box of crayons and an activity-filled placemat that is divided into word games,

Figure 5-5   Children's menu contest entry form (courtesy of Cafe Flavors, Charlotte, NC)

puzzles, a menu, and a drawing of a bear with the accompanying instructions: "Color in our bear, fill in the entry blank and hand this placemat to the cashier on your way out. A winner will be chosen each month. Winner will be notified by mail." (See Figure 5–6.)

The child who wins first place at each of the restaurants receives

**WIN A PRIZE FOR YOUR PICTURE!**

Color in our Bear, fill in the entry blank and hand this placemat to the cashier on your way out. A winner will be chosen each month. Winner will be notified by mail.

Name _____

Address _____

_____

_____

Birthday _____

Figure 5-6   Coloring contest menu (courtesy of Stern's, Paramus, NJ)

This card is good for
ONE FREE SUNDAE
and
A BIRTHDAY SURPRISE BOX.

To receive your free gifts,
**BRING THIS CARD** to any of
these Stern's Restaurants:
  Woodbridge Center, Woodbridge, N.J.
  Bergen Mall, Paramus, N.J.
  Willowbrook Mall, Wayne, N.J.
  Roosevelt Avenue, Flushing, N.Y.
  Broadway Mall, Hicksville, N.Y.
  Sunrise Mall, Massapequa, N.Y.

This card expires _____.

# STERN'S

Figure 5-7    Birthday invitation (courtesy of Stern's, Paramus, NJ)

a complimentary lunch, a special ice cream sundae, and a $10 gift certificate toward any store purchase. All other contestants are pronounced runners-up and are entitled to a free sundae upon their next restaurant visit.

There is one more facet to the program, according to Rena Levy, director of foodservices. She said, "The entry form not only asks for names and addresses, but we also request birthdates. From this information, we automatically enroll the children in our birthday club."

A few weeks prior to their birthdays, children are mailed a card inviting them back to the restaurant to celebrate with a free ice cream sundae. (See Figure 5–7.) As part of the package, they are also entitled to a "birthday surprise box" filled with plastic trinkets, including an animal-shaped spoon, an animal-shaped comb, and an animal-studded straw.

"We're letting everyone know that children are welcome here," said Levy. "When children are happy, mothers are happy, and they will come back."

## JUST A PENNY A POUND—PAY WHAT YOU WEIGH

The Ground Round has come full circle in its efforts to appeal to families with children.

When the first full-service restaurant opened in a converted Howard Johnson's in Norridge, Illinois, in 1969, families were the original targets. They came for the food, which was basically burgers. They came for the prices, which were moderate. They came for the atmosphere, which was relaxed. They came for the free peanuts, and for the rare privilege of being able to throw the shells all over the dining room floor.

The fun, informal concept proved successful, and by 1975 the chain had grown to 63 units. But the days of peanut crunching were numbered due to changes in health and fire codes. In the early 1980s many of the restaurants banned peanuts completely and converted into fern bars.

Later that same decade, recognizing the profit potential of baby boomers passing into parenthood, Braintree, Massachusetts-based Ground Round Restaurants, Inc. focused its attention on this rapidly growing segment. By 1990 newly appointed president and chief executive officer Michael O'Donnell pledged to turn the 156 company-owned and 44 franchised units into the nation's premier family dinnerhouse chain, according to Judith Kelly, vice president of marketing.

A new positioning statement speaking directly to families with children debuted in advertisements, announcing the Ground Round as a place "Where Kids Can Relax . . . and Grown-ups Can Have Fun."

Moving full steam ahead on the family track also called for intensified efforts to merchandise "Kids Pay What They Weigh Just a Penny a Pound" promotion that has been in existence for several years.

The great weigh-in—on old-fashioned scales displayed in all of the restaurants—is held once or twice a week, depending on traffic and individual markets. The average child, who takes advantage of the promotion rather than pay the $2.49 full price for a meal from the children's menu, weighs 61 pounds and so eats for 61 cents, according to Kelly.

"The payoff is that children this age don't come alone," she said. "It's really a brilliant promotion because it offers value to the parents and something out of the ordinary for the kids. From this great foundation, we're also able to build line extensions."

One variation on the theme, designed to spur seasonal sales, is the Kids Pay by Degree program, which runs from the first week in December through Christmas. Then, on Father's Day, it's dad's turn to pay what he weighs—at three cents per pound.

"In addition to major advertising and promotional considerations, there are a lot of little details that go into creating an environment conducive to family dining pleasure," adds Kelly. In this category falls everything from changing tables in both the men's and women's bathrooms to bendable straws making it easier for kids to sip their drinks.

To keep comfort levels high, children are always greeted with their own menus, their own set of cellophane-wrapped crayons displaying Ground Round's logo, and their own special placemats featuring activities with environmental messages. They are seated together with their families in the dining room while a separate lounge area typically caters to adult-only parties. Infants have their own special high chairs, designed to accommodate car seats. Servers are instructed to speak directly to kids and to bring out their meals as soon as they are ready.

Now families account for 46 percent of Ground Round's customers. They come for the food, which covers the palate profile. They come for the prices, which are still moderate. They come for the silent cartoons playing continuously on a big screen. They come for the restaurant's mascot, Bingo the Clown, who makes frequent guest appearances. Instead of peanuts, they come for the complimentary bowls of popcorn that are brought immediately to the table to satiate children's appetites until their meals are served.

## KIDS EAT FREE

Frankenmuth is a tiny dot on the Michigan map, approximately a 90-minute drive north of the Motor City. But every year more than one million visitors flock to the town for finger-lickin' "Zehnders of Frankenmuth's World Famous Family Style Chicken Dinners."

The all-you-can-eat feast, served in the 1,300-seat dining room, starts with homemade noodle soup, cabbage salad with sour cream dressing, cheese spread with garlic toast, chicken liver pate, old-fashioned white and stollen breads, large curd cottage cheese, and seasonal relish. Dressing, creamy mashed potatoes, giblet gravy, buttered egg noodles, garden vegetable, and choice of coffee, tea, or milk accompany the crispy, golden fried entree. There's ice cream for dessert—all for the price of $11.75. Children ages two to five are charged $3.50. Those ages six to eight pay $5.50 and those nine to 11, $6.50. The one exception is that all children 11 and under eat free when accompanied by an adult ordering dinner throughout January.

"Traditionally, January was our slowest month of the year. We also found that parents were looking for something to do with their children after coming down from the holidays. So we started 'January Is Children's Month at Zehnders' 10 to 15 years ago to generate traffic and create some excitement," said Bill Parlberg, vice president of operations.

The promotion is advertised in newspapers and cross-marketed in newsletters that are published quarterly by the operation.

A similar strategy—luring customers with kids' freebies—is proving equally successful at Hutchinson, Kansas-based Sirloin Stockade International. But rather than one entire month of free meals, the 77-unit chain has reserved one day a week.

"We love kids, but the truth is that they don't have any money to spend. Our motivating factor in starting the 'Kids Eat Free on Tuesday' program was to get kids to want to visit the restaurant and bring their paying parents, grandparents, aunts, and uncles with them," said Darald Linn, director of marketing. "We also wanted to boost this midweek dinner daypart."

Linn estimates that approximately 70 percent of the moderately priced family steakhouses lining the Mid-America landscape participate in the promotion. "Just seven of our stores are company-owned. The remainder are franchisees and they have the option to do what they wish," said Linn. "I can tell you that those that do choose to run the program are packed out on Tuesdays."

Any child 12 years or younger may order from the kids' menu— a selection ranging from hamburgers to chicken strips to corn dogs. Or they may visit the SmorgasBar, stocked with special kids' treats every Tuesday, including pizza, nachos, and meat sauce-topped spaghetti.

"The food bar also comes with a free desert bar, which includes soft-serve ice cream, plus a variety of toppings, plus cakes and candy. The kids love it."

## STRAIGHT A'S PROGRAM

Plata Grande, an upscale Mexican dinnerhouse chain owned by Carrollton Enterprises of Beltsville, Maryland, is making the grade with families by promoting the Straight A's program.

All students, from primary grades through college, who score straight A's during the school year qualify for a free meal any Sunday during the month of July. The meals may be ordered off the children's menu, or they may consist of any appetizer, entree, dessert, and beverage from the regular menu for an average ticket price of $11.

"We give away thousands of meals at a cost of several thousand dollars," said Nick Sikalis, general manager of the Calverton, Maryland location. "But where it comes into paying off is in the long-term gain. We're building future business for years to come."

Report cards are required as proof of academic excellence. They are reviewed by restaurant managers, who initial those that pass and heartily congratulate the kids and their families. According to Sikalis, "We try to keep it fair. Straight A's are not required in all subjects, just the majors: science, math, English, and social studies.

"The idea developed in 1984 and 1985 when families seemed to be coming together more and more," Sikalis added. "We started brainstorming on how to increase our involvement with the community and the kids. Straight A's is one way to inform students, especially the younger ones, that their accomplishments are being rewarded and that other people outside of their families are interested in their achievements."

Before initiating the program, Plata Grande contacted faculty and administration of area schools. Response was favorable and with the assurance that schools would advocate the offer to parents, Straight A's got underway.

The program is advertised in school publications and the local media, plus promoted in the restaurant on tabletents, which change every year. The Maryland State School Board has also helped the operation gain notoriety by citing its efforts in promoting good grades.

## FUTURE PIZZA MAKERS OF AMERICA

In seeking a generous slice of the youth market pie, Edwardo's Natural Pizza, a 22-unit chain owned by Mid-Continent Restaurants of Hillside, Illinois, created the "Future Pizza Makers of America" program.

School groups and scout troops of up to 30 children are invited behind-the-scenes to tour the kitchen of their local Edwardo's and participate in making their own pizzas. The field trips, targeted to children five to 10 years of age, are usually conducted early in the morning, before the restaurant opens, or in midday during downtime.

"We focus on kitchen safety and nutrition and talk about the four basic food groups. Then we review pizza-making rules, such as good pizza makers always wash their hands when they're in the kitchen and never touch machines without adult consent," said Kelly Magallanes, field marketing manager. She added, "Children get to eat the pizza that they make. Then we give them a cookie and a certificate stating that they are a 'Future Pizza Maker of America.'

"There is no charge to any of the groups. It's just something nice that we like to do. We get to meet the kids, and give them the food that they love."

## MATH BY THE SLICE

Godfather's Pizza now delivers a very distinctive product to elementary school classrooms across America. It's a unique math kit that comes packed in the Omaha, Nebraska-based chain's official pizza box, and features such elements as a high-quality, laminated pizza gameboard, topped with problems spelled out on cardboard pepperonis.

A panel of elementary school educators commissioned by Godfather's originally developed the teaching aid for students in Grades 2 through 5. Their objective was to stimulate interest in math and develop fundamental addition, subtraction, multiplication, and division skills. Godfather's ulterior motive was to establish loyalty with future paying customers.

There are instructive games to play, work sheets to fill out, and an incentive for performing well. For achieving a certain level of expertise, teachers reward students with a certificate redeemable for a small Godfather's pizza. (See Figure 5–8.)

"Our payback is that when kids receive the certificates, they will bring their families in to their local Godfather's for a celebration," said Steve Frisbie, public relations manager of the 525-unit chain. "It's a win-win situation. Math is more fun and students are learning in spite of themselves. Parents like it. Teachers like it. And we're benefiting from the positive public relations."

Other than on the certificate and the exterior packaging, Godfather's shied away from spreading its name all over the kit. "Teach-

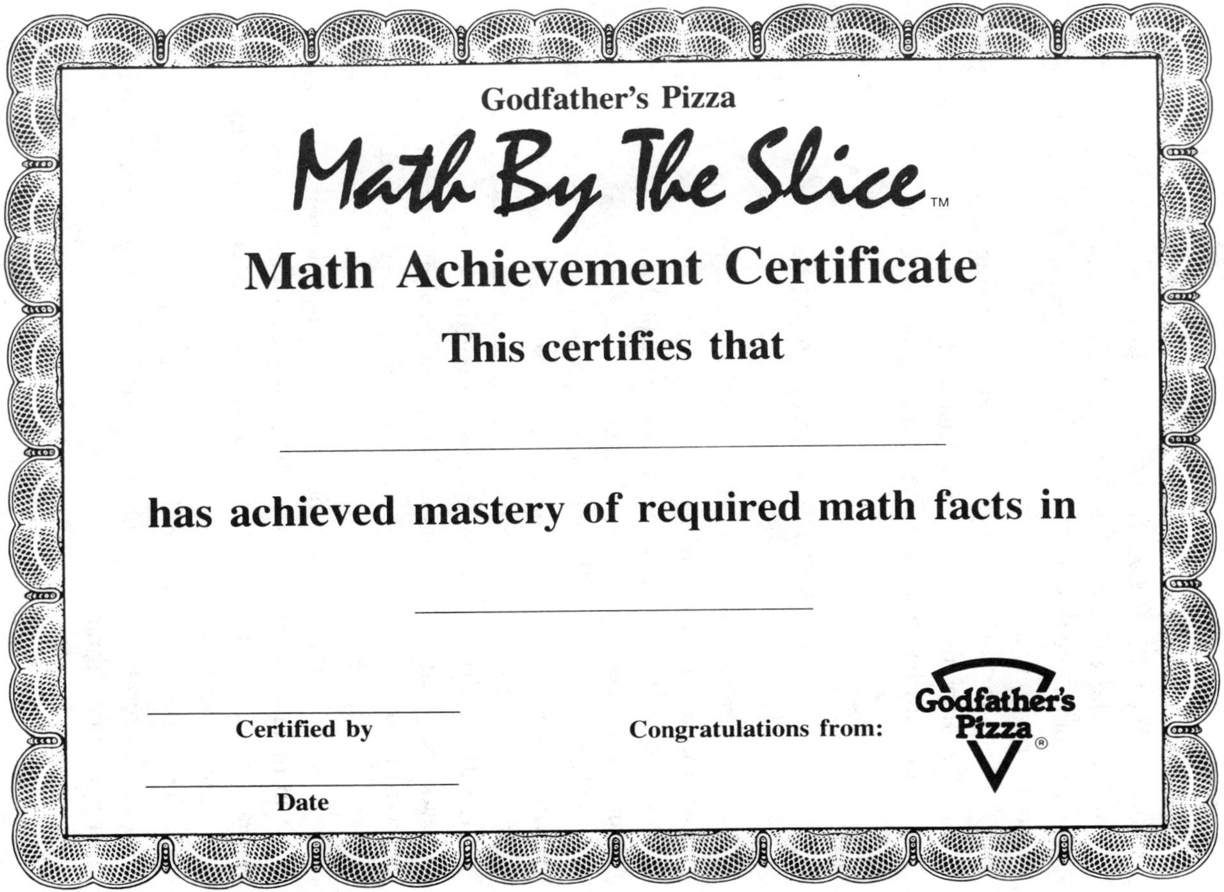

Godfather's Pizza

# *Math By The Slice*™

## Math Achievement Certificate

### This certifies that

_____

has achieved mastery of required math facts in

_____

Certified by _____

Date _____

Congratulations from:

Godfather's Pizza®

Figure 5-8  Godfather's Pizza Math Achievement Certificate
(courtesy of Godfather's Pizza, Inc., Omaha, NE)

ers can smell a rip-off from a mile away. They don't like overcommercialization.

"Response to Math by the Slice has been overwhelming," Frisbie added. "We fulfilled over 6,000 requests the first year that we mass produced the kits and made them available to franchisees to distribute free of charge to schools outside the Omaha area. Another 2,000 are on back order.

"They are fairly expensive to produce, costing us about $10 per kit. But franchisees are coming back and purchasing more because the program has been so successful in generating business."


## KING'S HONOR ROLL

Children are treated royally at King's Restaurant in Kinston, North Carolina, according to owner Wil King. In fact, they are courted in two separate programs sponsored by the 1,000-seat home of "world famous" barbecue pork and chicken.

"King's Honor Roll," which recognizes the area's best students with a free meal, is still going strong some six years after being introduced at school assemblies by the restaurant's mascot, a stuffed pig called Chitlings. Teachers are encouraged to select their best 12-years-and-younger students at the end of each grading period, and award them a certificate for a complimentary meal at King's. However, exactly what constitutes "best" is left up to teachers to decide. Said King, "Maybe it is someone overcoming a learning disability or an underachiever who is really making an effort. We want to let teachers use us as a tool to motivate all students to strive for academic excellence."

From this brain pool, a drawing is held at the end of the school year. The top prize is a book presented in the winner's name to his or her school library.

As the honor enrollees continue to grow, so do the number of free meals that King lavishes upon the young. But he can't complain. "It's rare that a kid will come in to claim a free meal without a parent or other brother or sister," he said. "The program brings us

Figure 5-9   Kids' Klub Kash Bucks promotion (courtesy of King's Restaurant, Kinston, NC)

new customers and gives us another shot with old customers that we haven't seen in a long time."

Chitlings has also become a real celebrity in the community, advancing King's name in the public eye.

Part Two to King's kids' story is the "King's Kids' Klub," which is open to any child 12 years of age or younger. Members get a card, a free birthday lunch or dinner, plus unlimited free mileage on Sweeney Snout, a mechanical pig who lives in a corner of the restaurant. Any child who presents his or her card after purchasing a meal also receives "Kids' Klub Kash Bucks," which can be redeemed for merchandise at the "King's Kids' Klub Korner." (See Figure 5-9.) Prizes range from bubbles to Barbie Dolls to basketballs and baseball gloves and are priced from one to 25 Bucks. They are displayed on shelves that are clearly marked so children know exactly how much items cost.

"We're encouraging savings, and we're encouraging coming back to King's," said King. "When you consider that approximately 50 percent of the time children are making the decision where to eat, we think a program aimed at increasing frequency is a very good thing for us. Parents love it because they feel that they've got to feed their kids somewhere. Why not come to King's?"

## PEASANT RESTAURANTS GO TO THE HEAD
## OF THE CLASS

Rather than sitting back, passing the time, waiting for customers to walk through the door, one multiconcept operator in Atlanta, Georgia, is actively reaching out to the community, recruiting a strong future base by developing partnership programs in city schools.

For nearly a decade, Peasant Restaurants—with 20-some restaurants primarily in the Atlanta, Baltimore, and Washington, D.C., areas—has supported the Adopt-a-School program, sponsored by the Atlanta Partnership of Business and Education, Inc. for Atlanta public schools.

Involvement was minimal at first. After being assigned an elementary school, the operators sat down with administrators and educators to formulate a mutually beneficial relationship.

"We were informed that the fifth grade holds an annual bake sale, and we were asked to donate desserts," said Stephan Nygren, president and founder of Peasant Restaurants. "Obviously, the program was designed to do more. So we met again with the principal and teachers to determine how we could really make a difference."

What resulted is a highly successful, nine-week course designed for 10- and 11-year-olds called "Owning a Bake Shop." For one hour each week, select representatives from Peasant Restaurants' staff instruct students in their classroom on subjects ranging from financial planning to restaurant design, training, and operations. After a behind-the-scenes field trip to one of the Peasant Restaurants to study computer systems, baking techniques, and how to order supplies, the fifth-graders set up their own shop.

They acquire a loan from the PTA. They develop a creative marketing strategy and publicity program. They work on staffing and develop a theme. They come up with a name for their enterprise and a menu. Then they design and build the booth to sell their sweet wares at the annual spring fair.

Peasant Restaurants still donates many of the desserts, and freely gives of its staff's time, which amounts to relatively small sacrifices compared to the program's awareness-building benefits.

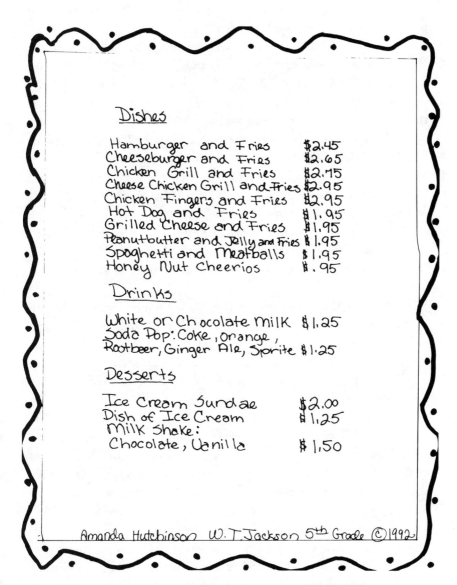

Figure 5-10   Mick's menu by kids (courtesy of Peasant
Restaurants, Atlanta, GA)

"In addition, we stimulate kids' interest in foodservice. We give them a practical approach to running a business. We give them real hands-on experience," said Nygren.

"We do a lot of community services in support of the arts and the prevention and treatment of diseases," he added. "But we get more back from what we do for the schools than from any other programs. It's rare that I'll be in a public setting, and won't be thanked by parents, grandparents, and kids for our involvement." Perhaps the ultimate honor has been receiving the Governor's Award for "Best Atlanta Partnership for Business and Education."

Nygren's advice for working with schools is to give the principal and teachers the respect they deserve, find out what their needs are, and tailor a program that's beneficial to them.

By taking this approach, Peasant Restaurants succeeded in instituting a second partnership venture with city schools. This time around, the subject is menu design, specifically for Mick's restaurant.

"Mick's is the 1990s answer for baby boomers who made fern bars popular in the 1980s, got married, had kids, then found no restaurant catering to them," said Nygren. It's casual. Prices are moderate. Parents feel comfortable bringing children.

The only thing lacking was a kids' menu. But what should it look like? Based on the positive experiences of the bake shop program, Nygren returned to the experts in the fifth grade to find out.

Now, a different school's art class is targeted each year for a five-to eight-week course focused on creating a menu for Mick's. Students are treated to a field trip and lunch at the restaurant to give them a feel for the ambience and a taste of the food. They are instructed to include a specific list of items, complete with prices. Then it's up to them to decide what they want their menu masterpieces to look like: the type or printing style, the layout, the colors, and the cover design. Since each student works individually, by the end of the school year, Mick's is the recipient of 20 to 30 original creations all signed by the artists. (See Figure 5–10.)

"The quality is great," said Nygren. "Plus, it's a great marketing tool. Kids bring in their whole families, including aunts, uncles, and cousins, to ask for their menus."

# Chapter Six

# *Celebrating Special Occasions*

When both heads of a household with children dive into the labor pool, the race against the clock suddenly speeds up. Days spent at work and evenings occupied with family business leave little time for daily get-togethers around the dining room or kitchen table, let alone planning and pulling off holiday feasts and special occasion celebrations. Seeking convenience, consumers are increasingly eating and entertaining outside of the home.

Opportunity knocks loud and clear for creative operators who have the space, staff, and stamina to handle the extra workload. In addition to major holidays, children's birthday parties and staged special events provide unlimited opportunities to ring up sales.

## SUNDAY IS FAMILY DAY

Start building a reputation as a destination dining spot by offering a family brunch on Sundays and holidays. Interest generated could bring expanded traffic the rest of the year.

- Offer a self-serve buffet table, scaled down just for kids and featuring an array of their favorite foods.
- Establish a theme, coordinating table decorations to attract attention to the children's station. If you have the resources,

consider setting up an electric train as a centerpiece. Or position the table under a brightly colored, striped tarp to create a circus atmosphere, complete with a clown serving fresh popcorn. Or design a zoo scene with stuffed animals spread out across the table. The more dramatic the setting, the more memorable the meal. At the very least, adorn the table with festive bouquets of helium-filled balloons. Each hour, stage a raffle and award a bouquet to the winner.

- Price the children's brunch so it represents a good value to parents. Charge half off the adult price, at least. Then try to benefit from carryover brunch business.

At Dingbats, one of seven multiconcept restaurants owned by Food Services Management Associates of Pittsburgh, Pennsylvania, children eat for free. "The kids are welcome at the adult buffet, but many of them prefer a special, smaller buffet. The knee-high table is skirted in cartoon character fabric and features foods that have special appeal to them, such as chicken fingers, pizza, M&M cookies, gingerbread men, and chocolate pudding," said Marlene Parrish, director of marketing.

During the rest of the day, all items on the kids' menu are priced at just 99 cents.

Sfuzzi, a chain of casual, contemporary restaurants based in Dallas, Texas, is doing well by following up brunch with its Sunday family dinner, featuring a specially priced menu of items served family-style on pass-around platters.

- Some additional dishes to consider featuring on the kids' brunch spread include yogurt (offered with a selection of mix-ins, such as sprinkles, chopped raisins, chopped peanuts, fruit cocktail in natural juice, etc.), mini-bagels with cream cheese, mini-biscuits with ham, cut up crisp vegetables, seasonal fruit, gelatin, macaroni and cheese, mini-franks and beans, spaghetti and meatballs, single-serving pot pies, single-serving pizzas, and, for dessert, homemade peanut butter and oatmeal raisin cookies.

- On holidays, such as Easter and Halloween, encourage front-of-the-house staff to dress up in costumes. Be a real hero by booking the Easter Bunny or Santa Claus and have them stop in to distribute jelly beans and candy canes, respectively, to the young diners.

- On days when you know that business will be brisk, such as Mother's Day, rent television sets and VCRs, and show videos during mealtime.

    "That way the kids can eat, then plop down in front of the TV while the parents finish at a more leisurely pace," said Parrish.

- Hire a magician, juggler, or clown, skilled at transforming balloons into recognizable shapes.

- Create a "free zone" where kids are at liberty to engage in independent and quiet play. Set up activities in a corner of the dining room within view of parents and out of the way of servers. Some items to stock include blocks, books, coloring books and crayons, puppets, dolls, and toy cars.

## PARTY PACKAGES

With time such a precious commodity, two-paycheck families are increasingly seeking convenient settings outside the home for their children's birthday parties. Restaurants that offer some element of play or diversion are in particularly good shape to capitalize on this market.

At Abate, another restaurant in the Food Services Management Associates' chain, pizza-making parties are a big hit with small fry.

At Leona's, a family-owned, mid-priced Italian restaurant chain in Chicago, Illinois, child revelers are treated to a puppet show, held every Saturday at one of the units.

At the Original Gino's East of Chicago, pizza party goers create a mural for the birthday boy or girl on a large sheet of plain paper hung by the staff.

Here are some additional food- and action-oriented party ideas for those attracted to the profit potential in this sideline occupation.

- Feature a sundae-making party. Scoop out ice cream, soft-serve, or frozen yogurt into individual dishes. Then, in a private room or secluded area of the restaurant, set up a soda fountain station with a variety of toppings. And let the fun begin!

- Offer a sub sandwich-making party, following basically the same procedure. Give children their own submarine rolls, and let them make their sandwiches from a selection of ingredients.

- Back to gooey desserts. One sure-fire recipe for success is to offer a workshop on cake decorating. Bring the kids back to the kitchen after lunch, and demonstrate how to transform cakes into works of art. Let older children have the hands-on experience of making their own creations by experimenting on cupcakes.

- Offer a tea for tots. Open the dining room during the hours of 2 P.M. to 4 P.M. or 3 P.M. to 5 P.M., when the restaurant is relatively empty. Serve a simple menu, such as peanut butter and jelly sandwiches cut in cookie cutter shapes, mini-chocolate chip scones, and fresh fruit cups. Instead of tea, pour warm cider or spiced apple juice. Then appoint someone on staff to conduct a brief etiquette lesson. Demonstrate how to set the table properly, how to fold napkins, when to use which fork and which spoon.

- Hotels can appeal to big spenders by promoting pajama parties. Include in the kids' overnighter a suite, pizza, beverages, and a birthday cake delivered by room service, along with full use of the hotel facilities. Set a limit on the age and number of attendees, making sure an adult will be supervising full-time.

- Do absolutely nothing except rent out space. Two Boots in New York City, New York brings in $25 an hour by making its private party room available to kids.

"We used to have children's parties in the restaurant, but we ran into trouble trying to control those three years old and younger," said Janet Henry, manager of the Italian-Cajun eatery. "In the party room, they can make their own noise, play games, race around. They usually order pizza and juice from us, but they can bring in whatever they want."

## COME TO THE AID OF EVERY PARTY

To make sure parties progress without a hitch, assign one person on staff as the key contact. Direct all inquiries to this special events liaison, whose basic responsibilities include the following.

- If more than one party is scheduled per day, properly time each function so there is no danger of overlap. (Most children's parties last two hours, maximum.)
- Confirm in writing, if possible, the time, date, number of guests, menu, and schedule of events promised each party giver.
- Require a down payment to hold reservations.
- Fully brief front-of-the-house staff on planned parties.
- Coordinate the menu with the kitchen.
- Oversee activities on the day of the party to make sure everything runs smoothly.

## SPECIAL OCCASIONS JUST FOR KIDS

Parties don't stop with the major holidays. For children, any day is as good as the next to stage an event. Any reason will do to call all young customers to a celebration.

- It's backwards day! Set aside one day a month, and offer lunch and dinner items at breakfast (soup, spaghetti) and special breakfast items for lunch and dinner. Just for kids, feature an eye-opener pizza (prepared with scrambled eggs, melted cheese, and ham or bacon on an open-faced English muffin spread with tomato sauce), silver dollar or teddy bear pancakes, pigs in the blanket (pancakes wrapped around sausage links), and/or French toast sticks.

- It's the snowiest (or driest) winter on record! Offer a "snowball" fest to drum up business during February. With each kids' meal sold, include a free scoop of vanilla ice cream rolled in coconut.

- Mom or dad gets a day off from work. Kids are entitled to a free lunch on Saturdays when accompanied by a parent.

- March is National Nutrition Month. Shake up sales by introducing healthy fruit-juice based drinks, garnished with fresh fruit and served with plastic, reuseable silly straws, which children get to take home.

- It's opening day at the ball park. Any kid customer coming in wearing a baseball cap receives a free pack of baseball cards, plus a scoop of bubble gum ice cream.

- During the Dog Days of August, set up a hot dog toppings bar. Some items to include, in addition to catsup and mustard, are baked beans, pickles, chopped tomatoes, thin slices of cucumbers, red and green pepper strips, nacho cheese sauce, and chili.

- Back to school is a big day. Go a little out of your way to cheer up children—and keep your restaurant top of mind—by passing out pencils, imprinted with your name and/or logo. Offering them in jazzy colors increases the chances that they will be used.

## MARK YOUR CALENDARS

There are many approaches you can use to take your operation to the top of customers' "A" entertainment and party lists. Here's a sample of some red letter days that are helping to turn the bottom line black for operators around the country.

## SFUZZI SFAMILY SFEAST

Leave it to an Italian restaurant chain to revive the American ritual of Sunday supper. Sfuzzi, Inc., headquartered in Dallas, Texas, conceived of the idea to switch over to family-style service every Sunday night in an attempt to increase traffic during "traditionally our weakest meal period," said Steve Singer, corporate executive chef. "We also thought that this value-oriented program would target families and children, who were absent from our clientele."

To spread the word, tabletents and a direct mail piece were created, touting "Sfuzzi Sfamily Sfeast" as "Sunday Sfun for Everyone" with "Lotsa Pasta for Not a Lotsa Money" and, another draw, "Kids under Twelve Complimentary." (See Figure 6–1.)

The occasion called for Chef Singer to develop a special menu of reasonably priced appetizer, entree, and dessert platters that could be ordered in portions for two, four, six, or more, passed around the table, split, and shared.

Children preferring to start with something other than "Baked Eggplant, Roma Tomatoes, Smoked Mozzarella, and Basil" or a main course of "Grilled Chicken Breast with Goat Cheese, Spinach, and Herb Risotto," may order from the kids' menu. (See Figure 6–2.)

The kids' selection, which is printed on a mask, includes "Romano Crusted Chicken Fingers with Honey Mustard Dipping Sauce" ($3.75); "Turtle-Shaped Raviolis with Ricotta Cheese and Tomato Sauce" ($3.25); "Basghetti (also known as Spaghetti) with Veal Meatballs" ($3.50); or "Just Cheese Pizza with No Vegetables! No Tomatoes! and No Funny Green Stuff!" ($3.50).

Business has been brisk at all 14 Sfuzzis staging the Sfunday Sfamily Sfeast.

## EASTER EGG HUNT

On Easter Sunday in New York City, 300-seat America is a restaurant where business really multiplies. Customers in their Easter best are escorted to tables by Easter Bunny-clad staff. But before they are

```
┌─────────────────────────────────────────┐
│                                           │
│       S U N D A Y   I S                   │
│                                           │
│       S F E A S T   D A Y                 │
│                                           │
│       A T   S F U Z Z I                   │
│                                           │
│                                           │
│   SHARE IN THE ITALIAN TRADITION OF FAMILY STYLE │
│                                           │
│   DINING. ABUNDANT FOOD. GREAT VALUE. FAMILY SERVICE. │
│                                           │
│   START THE DAY WITH SUNDAY BRUNCH AT ONLY │
│                                           │
│   $14.50 OR JOIN US ON SUNDAY NIGHTS FOR  │
│                                           │
│   TRADITIONAL ITALIAN STYLE DINING, WHICH IS, │
│                                           │
│   FAMILY STYLE. ENJOY APPETIZERS AND ENTREES │
│                                           │
│   SERVED ON LARGE PLATTERS MEANT FOR SHARING, │
│                                           │
│   WHETHER FOR TWO, FOUR, SIX OR MORE. ON  │
│                                           │
│   SUNDAYS CHILDREN UNDER 12 ARE COMPLIMENTARY. │
│                                           │
│       BRUNCH 10:30-3   DINNER 5-10        │
│                                           │
│                                           │
│   1800 POST OAK BOULEVARD  622-9600       │
│                                           │
└─────────────────────────────────────────┘
```

Figure 6-1    Sfuzzi Sfamily promotion (courtesy of Sfuzzi, Inc., Dallas, TX)

even seated, children are hopping over to the bar to hunt for Easter eggs.

"The annual Easter egg hunt has become a tradition," said Michael Weinstein of multiconcept conglomerate Ark Restaurants, owner of America as well as 25 other eateries. In recalling how the event came about, Weinstein said, "We try to be sensitive to the space and the neighborhood that we are in. At America, we were seeing more and more families starting to use the restaurant. So we decided if that's how people wanted to use it, we'd do things to help them along.

"The first thing we did was hire a sleight-of-hand magician to work all day Saturday and Sunday. Then, during December, we brought in Santa to meet with children and go over their Christmas lists."

The Easter egg hunt was a logical move, given the unique layout of the restaurant and bar area, which is actually a 2,000 square foot platform situated in the rear center of the dining room. The space lends itself to being sectioned off, covered entirely in plastic grass, and strewn with Easter eggs, hand-painted by members of the staff.

Hunts are held throughout the day. As soon as all the eggs are scooped into baskets, children are asked to clear the floor. More

Figure 6-2    Sfuzzi kids' menu (courtesy of Sfuzzi, Inc., Dallas, TX)

eggs are laid down, and new children are invited to play. Those who find hollowed out eggs are treated to a little surprise. Two Easter Bunny helpers are employed by the restaurant to assist children in their search.

"We do it (the event) for goodwill, so it's hard to measure how much business it actually brings in," said Weinstein. He estimates serving some 1,000 kids on that special Sunday and satisfying them 100 percent since "the only problem is they never want to leave."

The real beauty of the promotion is that it helps build family business year-round, Weinstein added.

## A BIG HIT WITH LITTLE KIDS

Another New York City-based multiconcept restaurant chain, Restaurant Associates, provides one more example of how to take advantage of a strategic location and special occasion.

The scene is the Broadway bastion of tomato sauce-smothered pasta and other Southern Italian delights, Mamma Leone's, which has been feeding families for 85 years. When the big Broadway hit, *The Secret Garden*, opened in the theater across the street and started playing to packed, family-filled audiences, a promotional tie-in was in order.

The press release launching the special kids-eat-free program announced, "Parents, grandparents, relatives, or friends who take a child to see the Broadway smash hit *The Secret Garden* can make it an even bigger treat with the new 'Kids Eat Free' menu at Mamma Leone's. Starting immediately, upon presentation of a ticket or ticket stub to any performance of *The Secret Garden*, kids eat free any weeknight when accompanied by an adult."

Each meal on the theme menu is named after a character or place in the play, such as "Mary Lennox . . . Mixed Fruit Salad," "House upon the Hill . . . Meatballs and Spaghetti," and "The Opening Dream . . . Boneless Breast of Chicken Parmigiana with Spaghetti." (See Figure 6–3.) The flip side features a picture of the secret garden to color, a find-the-word game, and a simple quiz (Q. Who is the youngest actress to ever win a Tony Award? A. Daisy Eagan, star of the show.)

"We expect *The Secret Garden* to run for years so we'll be feeding a lot of happy kids," said the restaurant's "Direttore Generale" Joe Montalbano.

Children are also catered to at Restaurant Associates' American Museum Restaurant in the American Museum of Natural History. At this locale, dinosaurs are the fitting theme of the "Junior Menu," geared toward the 10 and under set. (See Figure 6–4.) Selections include "Dino de la Pizza" and the "Meal-O-Saurus," featuring a quarter-pound hamburger with "Dino fries" and a "Dino toy." Dinosaur-shaped sugar candies and dinosaur juice containers, called "Dino Sippers," are also available.

## SUNDAY CHILDREN'S BRUNCH

The Wyndham Hamilton Hotel in Itasca, Illinois, has "the most renowned brunch in all of suburban Chicago," according to Lee Belfield, food and beverage director of the 408-room property. The food station reserved just for kids definitely is another claim to fame.

Items cycled through the children's Sunday spread range from French toast sticks to chicken fingers to pigs in the blanket. "Mini-pizzas are especially popular, particularly with dads, who we find going through the line, grabbing a few at a time," said Belfield. Gelatin, cookies, and brownies, cut in small portions, are also available.

"We want to serve food that kids will like, and parents will accept. Sometimes those are mutually exclusive goals," he said.

With the exception of baked goods, which are made on the premises, most other kid dishes tend to be purchased preprepared, which is a real labor saver.

The food is displayed on a table, distinguished by its short legs, colorful tablecloth, and small-scale cartoon characters positioned around the perimeter. "We dress it up for kids," said Belfield. To

Children's Complete Menu
$7.95
*Choose from:*

## Appetizers
*Mary Lennox*...Mixed Fruit Salad
*Dickon*...Slice of Fresh Melon

## Main Courses

*House Upon the Hill*...
Meatballs and Spaghetti

*Garden's Delight*...
Freshly Prepared Lasagne, Meat Sauce

*The Robin*...
Ravioli with Meat Sauce

*Show Me the Key*...
Fettucine - Alfredo or Meat Sauce

*The Opening Dream*...
Boneless Breast of Chicken Parmigiana
with Spaghetti

## Desserts
*Old Ben's Garden*...
Mamma's Special Ice Cream:
Chocolate, Vanilla, Strawberry
Pistachio, Cappuccino
Lemon Ice

*Kids eat free accompanied by a paying adult all weekend.*
*Kids eat free all week with a ticket stub from*
*"The Secret Garden" and accompanied by a paying adult*

Figure 6-3    Secret Garden Menu at Mamma Leone's, New York
City (courtesy of Restaurant Associates, New York, NY)

# MAMMA'S QUIZ

1. What is the Ninja Turtles favorite Italian food?
2. Which famous Broadway show is named after family pets?
3. Who is the fat cartoon cat born at Mamma Leone's and what is his favorite food?
4. Who is the youngest actress to ever win a Tony Award?
5. Which well-known red vegetable is also considered a fruit?
6. Which Broadway show is located across the street from Mamma Leone's?
7. What Italian meal did "The Lady and the Tramp" share in the Disney movie of the same name?
8. What is Mamma Leone's first name? (Hint: *check your parent's menu*)

8. Luisa

6. "The Secret Garden".....7. Spaghetti & Meatballs

4. Daisy Eagan "The Secret Garden".....5. A Tomato.....

1. Pizza.....2. "Cats".....3. "Garfield" & Lasagne

# JUNIOR MENU
### *(10 and under, please)*

## Dino de la Pizza
*An individual Pizza and Salad*
*with French Dressing*

## American "Moo"-Seum Classic
*Grilled American Cheese, French Fries*
*and Pickle*

## Children's Fruit Plate
## with Vanilla Yogurt

## Foot Long Hot Dog with Chips
## and Cole Slaw

## "MEAL-O-SAURUS"
*Quarter Pound Hamburger,*
*Dino Fries, Cole Slaw & a Pickle.*
*Served with a "Dino Toy."*

*Choice of*
## Soft Drink, Juice,
## Milk or Chocolate Milk

## 5.95

## DINO SIPPER 1.50
## DINO COOKIE .75

Figure 6-4   Junior menu from the American Museum of Natural History Restaurant (courtesy of Restaurant Associates, New York, NY)

# Trachodon

The Trachodon wants to get to the other side of the water. Help him find his way. Notice his feet and bili are just like a duck's.

make the selection process easier, "It's at their eye level too, although there are servers there to help."

Children five and under eat free. Those ages six to 12 are charged $9.95, about half the price an adult must pay.

When asked to put a figure on how much of the hotel's brunch business is attributed to kids, Belfield replied, "We can't assess that unless we stop the program—and we're not about to do that."

Across the country, the Four Seasons Clift Hotel, San Francisco, California, also has established a reputation for sumptuous Sunday brunch. The memorable spread for children is set up on a two-and-one-half-foot-tall buffet table and features a model train running through the elaborate display.

Obviously, major emphasis is placed on presentation, according to executive chef Kelly Mills. Children delight at the Tonka truck filled with potato chips and the American Flyer wagon loaded with Twinkees. Rounding out the selection are JELL-O, ready-to-eat pudding, hot dogs, chicken drumettes, and Kraft macaroni and cheese, "not some fancy chef creation with chevre," said Mills.

Brunch for adults costs $32.50. For children 12 and under, the all-inclusive price of $9 includes a store-quality coloring book and crayons or, if they prefer, a cuddly toy.

## PIZZA-MAKING PARTY

Baby boomers, who marked the passing of each year while growing up with a party, aren't about to deprive their children of the same quality experience. Let them celebrate birthdays with friends, play games, blow out candles, and open presents—as long as these festivities take place on somebody else's turf.

According to Marlene Parrish, director of marketing of Food Services Management Associates, Pittsburgh, Pennsylvania, high on the priority lists of today's busy parents are places to hold parties that offer convenience, trouble-free service, reasonable prices, and guaranteed fun.

Abate, one of seven restaurants owned by the multiconcept operator, fits the bill. Its "Make-Your-Own-Pizza" birthday party package includes personal pizzas, soft drinks, and birthday cake, plus gift-filled helium balloons for all party goers, all for $5.95 per person. It's easy, offbeat, and there's no mess for mom and dad to clean up. The restaurant manager handles all arrangements. In fact, parents are only responsible for sending out invitations and picking up the tab.

When the big day arrives, children file in to a private party room, with capacity for about 35 people. "But eight is the most reasonable number to work with," said Parrish.

"The room is completely secluded. We also display a great big bunch of balloons at the door, along with a sign that says party in progress." So there is no chance of being disturbed or of disrupting other diners.

The pizza makers are stationed at tables and given dough to pat out into pans. Then, toppings are personally selected and arranged in such a fashion so that there will be no mistaking whose pizza is whose. While the pies bake in the kitchen, it's time to play games and open gifts. As soon as the pizzas are done, the children get to eat them.

Parrish does some advertising in local parent-oriented publications. But word-of-mouth has been the best method of spreading the news of the pizza parties to potential prospects.

In addition to parties, Food Services Management employs several other tactics to encourage the family trade.

"Where there are kids, there are parents," said Marlene Parrish. "Because kids' preferences and needs are influential in the decision of a restaurant choice, a good part of our marketing strategy is targeted to seeking and pleasing the small fry market."

At Dingbats, a casual, midscale restaurant with four locations in the Pittsburgh area, all children upon seating receive a goodie bag containing an activity book, crayons, and an application to join the restaurant's birthday club. The activity books and crayons are purchased in bulk. Money saved is used to print special plastic bags bearing the restaurant's name and logo. "It's the kind of bag that you can hang on the lighter in the car, and use to collect trash," said Parrish.

During the week, the restaurants are open for school field trips.

Letters are sent to principals to inform them of the opportunity for students to take a behind-the-scenes tour of a professional kitchen, and watch the chef prepare Dingbats' signature dessert, Mudpie. "It's a glorious mess of cookie crumbs, ice cream, and chocolate sauce," said Parrish.

All day Saturday, free lunch is available for children at the downtown Dingbats, which is in a shopping complex. Come Sunday, brunch for kids is complimentary at all locations while lunch and dinner prices for kids' meals drop to 99 cents.

# DINING DIARY

*Kids Dine Out* began with a broad overview of the children's market. The statistics led into stories of how operators from coast to coast are reaching out to families and prospering from their business. Before closing the book, I thought it only fitting to turn the tables, so to speak, and spotlight what life's really like at dinnertime inside a child-filled household headed by a double bill of wage-earners.

The intent of this diary is to help you fully understand the critical role foodservice plays today in the lives of baby boomers and their broods. As you are about to discover, the relationship can best be described as codependent. You thrive on our business. We couldn't eat without you.

The "typical" family I've chosen to portray happens to be mine. In addition to myself, there's my husband, Gary, our eight-year-old son, Eli, our six-year-old daughter, Adrienne, and our infant, Gabriel. The events are entirely true, and occurred one week before *Kids Dine Out* was due at the publishers.

## Sunday

Because I was going to be working all day, Gary volunteered to stop at the market and pick up enough provisions to get us through the week. He left without a list, and returned with

- Three heads of lettuce
- One jar of pepperoncini salad peppers

- One gallon of milk (expiration date, the next day)
- One two-pound loaf of white bread
- From the deli counter, one-half pound of sliced turkey, an equal amount of sliced salami, and one-quarter pound of sliced baked ham

Needless to say, we went out for dinner that night, with the children, our daughter's friend, and her friend's father, choosing a Greek restaurant because:

- The menu is extensive enough to please everyone with something.
- It's noisy.
- The service is swift and highly professional.
- If you arrive early, there's rarely a wait.
- Prices are moderate.

Adrienne ordered avgolemono soup (chicken broth, egg yolks, lemon juice, and rice). Eli selected beef shish kebab. The baby had a bottle. Gary had roast chicken (just like my mother used to make). I split broiled whitefish with Adrienne's six-year-old friend (who also ate all the anchovies on the salad).

### Monday

Gary and I both had to be at meetings by 7:30 P.M.

Eli and Adrienne "feasted" on macaroni and cheese, courtesy of Kraft, and raw veggies while I prepared tuna salad for myself. Gary got home from the office too late to eat.

### Tuesday

I actually prepared a hot meal. We dined on chicken breasts that I'd found in the freezer, defrosted, then stuffed with mushrooms, spinach, and ham (a concoction that the children proceeded to pick out and remove to the polar regions of their plates), a salad, and buttered noodles.

### Wednesday

Domino's delivered two large pizzas, one topped with pepperoni for Gary and Adrienne, another topped with double cheese for Eli and mushrooms over half (for me).

### Thursday

The sitter stopped at McDonald's, picking up Happy Meals for Eli and Adrienne to consume at our dining room table. I met Gary downtown to see a play. The performance ran late, and we didn't have time to stop for an after-theater bite.

### Friday

Still haven't had time to go to the grocery store. The whole family, including Gary's father who was visiting from out of town, went out to eat. This time, we chose a casual restaurant specializing in Southern barbecue that we often frequent because:

- We all enjoy the food (kids love ribs, especially).
- It's noisy.
- The service is excellent.
- There's rarely a wait if you arrive early.
- Prices are moderate.

Sound familiar?

### Saturday

Went shopping!

# OPERATOR ROSTER

The following foodservice operations are featured in *Kids Dine Out*, and all fit the definition of being kid-friendly.

- They acknowledge children as a viable market.
- They are sensitive to kids' needs as well as to the needs of today's parents.
- They welcome the opportunity to serve families.
- They are succeeding in establishing loyalties early on to assure a strong customer base in the future.

Abate
Pittsburgh, PA

America
New York, NY

The American Cafe
Laurel, MD

American Museum Restaurant
New York, NY

The Angus Barn
Raleigh, NC

The Back Bay Rowing & Running Club
Costa Mesa, CA

Big Boy/Elias Brothers Restaurants, Inc.
Warren, MI

Bistro Banlieue
Lombard, IL

Bob's Burger Express, Inc.
Salem, OR

Boogie's Diner
Boulder, CO

Boulevard
New York, NY

Bub City Crabshack & Bar-B-Q
Chicago, IL

Burger King
Miami, FL

Cadillac Ranch
Bartlett, IL

Cafe Flavors
Charlotte, NC

Casey's Caboose
Killington, VT

Chi-Chi's
Woodbridge, NJ

Chili's Bar & Grill
Dallas, TX

Colors Cafe
Encinitas, CA

Country Kitchen
Minneapolis, MN

Delta Air Lines, Inc.
Atlanta, GA

Denny's
Spartanburg, SC

Dingbats
Pittsburgh, PA

Dumas Walter's
Mt. Prospect, IL

Eat 'n Park
Pittsburgh, PA

Ed Debevic's
Chicago, IL

Edwardo's Natural Pizza
Hillside, IL

Four Seasons Clift Hotel
San Francisco, CA

Fritz's Restaurant
Kansas City, KS

Frontera Grill
Chicago, IL

Godfather's Pizza, Inc.
Omaha, NE

The Ground Round, Inc.
Braintree, MA

Happy Joe's Superstore
Davenport, IA

The Hotel Hershey
Hershey, PA

Howard Johnson Restaurants/Franchise Associates, Inc.
South Weymouth, MA

Hyatt Hotels Corp.
Chicago, IL

King's Restaurant
Kinston, NC

Late for the Train
Menlo Park, CA

Leona's
Chicago, IL

Lyon's Restaurants, Inc.
Foster City, CA

Mamma Leone's
New York, NY

Mitzel's American Kitchen
Seattle, WA

Original Gino's East
Chicago, IL

Paul's Place
Denver, CO

Peasant Restaurants
Atlanta, GA

The Peddler
Gatlinburg, TN

A Piece of Quiet
Denver, CO

Plata Grande
Beltsville, MD

Port of Subs, Inc.
Reno, NV

Ramada International Hotels & Resorts
Phoenix, AZ

Robin's
Pasadena, CA

Rockwells American Restaurants
Scarsdale, NY

Royal Caribbean Cruises Ltd.
Miami, FL

Sfuzzi, Inc.
Dallas, TX

Sirloin Stockade International
Hutchinson, KS

Spago
West Hollywood, CA

Spangles
Brentwood, CA

Stern's
Paramus, NJ

T.G.I. Friday's
Dallas, TX

Two Boots
New York, NY

Walt Disney World Resort
Lake Buena Vista, FL

Wendy's International
Dublin, OH

The Westin La Paloma
Tucson, AZ

Wyndham Hamilton Hotel
Itasca, IL

Zehnders of Frankenmuth
Frankenmuth, MI

Zoopa
Seattle, WA

# FAMOUS LAST WORDS

To put the family market into perspective, here is a compilation of quotes contributed by operators featured in *Kids Dine Out*.

"In response from customers' requests, we started a kids' menu, and it's made the restaurant successful."

Stewart Rosen, Owner
Boulevard
New York, NY

"We're seeing a lot more working parents opt for four- and five-day vacations. Children are an integral part of their travel plans, and they've become important customers for us."

Ken Halligan, Food and Beverage Director
The Westin La Paloma
Tucson, AZ

"As you may know, the kids of today are the customers of tomorrow. Kids will influence their parents on their decision of where to dine."

From the Training Manual of Robin's
Robin Salzer, Owner
Pasadena, CA

"Families are the backbone of our business."

Rick Jones, General Manager
The Peddler
Gatlinburg, TN

"We realized a long time ago that children are the ones who decide where to eat. When we do get them in the restaurant, our main marketing objective is to treat them like gods."

John Berres, Owner
Cafe Flavors
Charlotte, NC

"We are sealing bonds with future customers (by catering to children). We try to do our best to create a family atmosphere and run the restaurant by people who care."

Rick Bayless, Owner
Frontera Grill/Topolobampo
Chicago, IL

"Families are a priority with us. We do everything we can to build loyalty and to get them to come into Godfather's."

Steve Frisbie, Manager, Public Relations
Godfather's Pizza
Omaha, NE

"People with young children traditionally had the least disposable income. Now this is changing rapidly. With the delay of childbirth, they have money, but less time. Where kids are going today are fast food and casual dining restaurants because that's where mom and pop went when they were dating. It works because they have the menus kids want."

Jon Ostrov, Vice President of Marketing
Country Kitchens International
Minneapolis, MN

"We've always been family oriented. But as competition for family dollars increased in recent years, we wanted to make sure we'd continue attracting this market."

Bob Schneden, Director of Public Relations
Happy Joe's Superstore
Davenport, IA

"Children are our future customers. We really cater to them."

William King, Owner
King's Restaurant
Kinston, NC

"We felt that offering this option (baby-sitting service) to our customers enhanced our image. Not only are we perceived as a friendly, casual, all-American restaurant, but also one with truly something for everyone—including the parents who deliberate between staying home and dragging children out for a less-than-relaxing dining experience. As a foodservice establishment, this also helps increase the traffic on particularly slow evenings."

Barbara Gentile, Restaurant Spokesperson
Rockwells American Restaurants
Westchester County, NY

"These kids are my future customers. We want this to be their destination restaurant."

Don Bruyn, General Manager
The Back Bay Rowing & Running Club
Costa Mesa, CA

"Our clientele changed considerably over a 15-year period. All of a sudden, yuppies were becoming young parents. We wanted to make sure that parents with small children felt welcome."

Julia Obici, Director of Marketing
The American Cafe
Laurel, MD

"People who are reluctant to hire baby-sitters are bringing their children to dine with us. We really haven't met a child so far that we haven't been able to please."

Van Eure, Owner
The Angus Barn
Raleigh, NC

# SOURCES

Here's a place to start shopping around for food, suppliers of premiums, menu planners, and merchandisers of kid-related items. The list is by no means complete. For more leads on how to complement your menu and create promotional programs with kid-related goods, check with your distributor.

## FUN FOODS

### Candy/Cereal/Cookies/Crackers

Kellogg Foodservice
One Kellogg Square
Battle Creek, MI 49016
616-961-2000

Lance Inc.
P.O. Box 32368
Charlotte, NC 28232
704-554-1421

*Crackers, nuts, chips, popcorn, snack cakes, and candy in portion-packs*

M&M/Mars
Division of Mars, Inc.

800 High Street
Hackettstown, NJ 07840
908-850-2784

*Portion-packaged chocolate-coated candy treats, plus a line of tabletop activity placemats*

Nabisco Foods Group
Food Service Division
7 Campus Drive
Parsippany, NJ 07054
201-682-6879

*Oreos, Teddy Grahams*

Sunshine Biscuits, Inc.
Foodservice Division
100 Woodbridge Center Drive
Woodbridge, NJ 07095-1196
201-855-4000

*Honey grahams, animal crackers, and Grahamy Bears™*

### Chicken

McCarty Foods, Inc.
P.O. Box 2718
Jackson, MS 39207
601-371-2700
800-647-2364

*Full line of breaded and unbreaded flavored chicken nuggets, patties, and fingers, including pizza flavor-glazed nuggets and patties and boneless drumsticks*

Perdue Farms Inc.
P.O. Box 1537
Salisbury, MD 21802
800-45-PERDUE

*Full line of poultry products, including boneless drumsticks and heart-shaped chicken nuggets*

Pierce Foods
Division of Hester Industries, Inc.
c/o Marketeam, Inc.
120 Bellview Avenue
Winchester, VA 22601
703-667-7710
800-336-9876

*Pierce Country Nuggets Galore™ in fun shapes, such as smile-shaped Hot Lips and Sweet Lips, heart-shaped Sweet Hearts, triangular Chik-Nachos, mini-Country Cubits, and zigzag-shaped Wirligigs*


## Fish & Seafood

Fishery Products International
18 Electronic Avenue
Danvers, MA 01923
508-777-2660

*Sea Wonders™ honey-flavored North Atlantic cod nuggets in five playful shapes: starfish, anchor, sea horse, fish, and shark*


## Pizza

Little Charlies Entree Division
115 West College Drive
Marshall, MN 56258
800-533-5290
In MN: 1-800-622-5200

*Mini-pizza bagels to heat in microwave or conventional ovens*


## Potatoes/Veggies:

The Clorox Company
1221 Broadway
Oakland, CA 94612
415-271-2909

*Moore's*™ *onion rings and appetizers, including pizza sticks, plus Kids'*
*Klub Kit available*

McCain Foods, Inc.
O'Hare Corporate Tower II
10600 West Higgins Road
Rosemont, IL 60018
708-297-3260

*Alphabet Fries*™ *and Dinosaurs & Things*™, *featuring fries in six*
*different shapes*

### Soup

Campbell Soup Company
Foodservice Division
Campbell Place
Camden, NJ 08103
609-342-4800

*Dinosaur and Souper Stars soups for kids*

### Yogurt

The Dannon Company, Inc.
1111 Westchester Avenue
White Plains, NY 10604
914-697-9700

*Dannon Sprinkl'ins*

## FURNITURE/DECOR

Midwest Tropical Inc.
3665 Lunt
Lincolnwood, IL 60645
708-679-6666

*Decorative aquariums*

Baby-Safe Commodities
204 High Street
P.O. Box 965
Jackson, OH 45640
614-286-8453

*Juvenile high chairs featuring custom laminated molded shell infant seats*

Safe-Strap Company, Inc.
30 Centre Road, Unit 2
Somersworth, NH 03878
603-692-6196
800-448-8945

*Safe-Sitter infant high chair accommodates sitting and sleeping positions, and features heavy-gauge aluminum frame on casters with two locking caster brakes*

Smart Products, Inc.
307-K West Tremont Avenue
Charlotte, NC 28203
704-347-0087
800-343-3635

*High chairs for infants featuring high-impact molded plastic, cushioned seats mounted on heavy-duty steel or decorative wood-finished frames that roll on casters, plus the SmartChair™ high chair for children*

## PREMIUMS AND PROMOTIONS

### *Balls/Balloons*

National Latex of California
P.O. Box 223643
Dallas, TX 75222-3643
213-544-3363
800-832-1515

*Toy balloons and playballs*

The Oak Rubber Company
219 South Sycamore Street
Ravenna, OH 44266-1203
216-296-3416

*Impact process imprinted balloons, Punch-O-Balls™ and sports balls, plus accessories*

Spir-it, Inc.
11 Lake Street
Wakefield, MA 01880
617-245-8700
800-343-0996

*Accessories for helium-filled balloons*

Windy Balloon Corporation
106 West Gardena Boulevard
Gardena, CA 90248
213-532-5353
800-421-1980

*Full line of balloons and accessories available in custom screen-print or stock designs*

## Cups

Alabaster Industries
Alabaster Premium Division
P.O. Box 429 Industrial Road
Alabaster, AL 35007
205-663-3836

*Full line of cups and mugs*

Aladdin Synergetics, Inc.
555 Marriott Drive, Suite 400
P.O. Box 100888
Nashville, TN 37210

615-748-3600
800-888-8018

*Foam-insulated cups and mugs*

Alpha Products Inc.
1455 Ellsworth Industrial Drive
Atlanta, GA 30318
404-351-3003

*Full line of cups and mugs, including Freeze 'n Go Mugs, Fizzy Lids, and Mini-Squeeze Bottles*

Betras Plastics Inc.
Highway 221 North at I-85
P.O. Box 6325
Spartanburg, SC 29304
803-599-0855
800-845-7027

*Full line of cups and mugs, including Nestable, 32-ounce sports bottles in licensed or custom-imprinted designs*

Countryside Products
A Division of Lynd Properties, Inc.
411 N. Reynoldsburg-New Albany Road
P.O. Box 12356
Columbus, OH 43213
614-861-6116
800-522-2340

*Extensive line of squeeze bottles to imprint with logo*

Cups Illustrated
2155 West Longhorn Drive
Lancaster, TX 75134
214-224-8407
800-334-CUPS

*Plastic souvenir cups, plus support services ranging from program design, Custom P.O.P kits, sports licensing, and floor-stocked inventory*

Inotec Corporation
526 North 700 West
North Salt Lake, UT 84054
801-298-4805

*No-tip, no-spill designed Floppy Cup™, made of flexible bag material attached to a rigid spout and cap, holds 34 ounces of liquid and comes with soft flexi-straw and 30-inch carrying string; custom printing available*

Letica Corporation Headquarters
1700 West Hamlin Road
P.O. Box 5005
Rochester, MI 48308-5005
313-652-0557
800-538-4221

*Maui Cup™ souvenir plastic drink cups, available in 16-, 21-, and 32-ounce sizes, with thermoformed or injection-molded lids*

Promotional Packaging Group
4547 Westgrove Drive
Dallas, TX 75248
214-713-9147
800-833-6490

*Cups, mugs, jugs, squeeze bottles, plus 32-ounce and 44-ounce "canteen coolers"*

Sweetheart Cup Company Inc.
7575 South Kostner Avenue
Chicago, IL 60652
312-767-3300

*Gallery™ souvenir cups and lids available in custom or numerous stock designs*

Whirley Industries, Inc.
618 Fourth Avenue
Warren, PA 16365
814-723-7600
800-825-5575

*Full line of cups and mugs to imprint with logo, including the Animug™ set: featuring color designs of dog, cat, tiger, and elephant topped with a hat-shaped lid and all-purpose plastic kids' box to use as a meal container*

## Menu and Promotion Planning/Packaging

Admark, Inc.
3630 SW Burlingame Road
Topeka, KS 66611
913-267-4712
800-677-4712

*Comprehensive line of stock and custom promotional cartons, premiums, and point-of-sale material*

Creative Menus Inc.
6059 South Oak Park Avenue
Chicago, IL 60638
312-586-3244

*Menu design and production*

Filet Menus
1830 South La Cienga Boulevard
Los Angeles, CA 90035
310-202-8000

*Menu design and production*

J&L Promotions
23675 Woodward Avenue

Pleasant Ridge, MI 48069
313-542-4700

*Customized kids' promotions planning*

Merlin Marketing, Inc.
428 Page Avenue, Suite 14
Atlanta, GA 30307
404-378-5745

*Four-color, fully illustrated cartons for kids' meals in Wildlife Adventure series (depicting penguins, harp seals, and bear cubs); Easter Bunny and Christmas collections (featuring Santa, elves, and snowmen)*

The New Kenyon Press, Inc.
12616 Chadron Avenue
Hawthorne, CA 90250
213-331-4500
800-752-9395

*Complete hospitality graphic services*

Promotions, Inc.
760 Transfer Road
St. Paul, MN 55114
612-642-1282
800-325-8511

*Custom kids' meal programs, with dozens of safety-tested, nonlicensed premiums available in a wide variety of price ranges*

Seattle Menu Specialists Inc.
5150 Russell Avenue NW
Seattle, WA 98107
206-784-2340
800-622-2826

*Menu design and production*

TPI Promotional Marketing
5950 Canoga, Suite 520
Woodland Hills, CA 91367
818-719-6530

*Sales promotion firm specializing in contests, sweepstakes, clubs, cross-promotions, games—a full range of services*

## Tabletop Products/Toys/Games/Placemats

Binney & Smith, Inc.
1100 Church Lane
P.O. Box 431
Easton, PA 18044-0431
215-253-6271

*Crayola crayons, washable crayons, chalkboard, sidewalk chalks, markers and washable markers, in bulk and cello-wrapped portion packs, plus a full line of placemats and die-cut puzzles*

Integra Development International
307 Canal Street
Lemont, IL 60439
708-257-8785

*Water-filled Splashies Placemats*

Mello Smello
5100 Highway 169 North
Minneapolis, MN 55428
612-537-8400
800-328-4876

*Line of scented stickers*

Mid-America Merchandising Inc.
204 West Third Street
Kansas City, MO 64105

816-471-5600
800-333-6737

*Awards, gifts, premiums, and incentives*

Neil Enterprises Inc.
940 Forest Edge Drive
Vernon Hills, IL 60061
708-913-8866
800-621-5584

*Snapins™ Kids Crafts keep children occupied with black-and-white panels to color in, then snap together in mugs, planters, keychains, magnets, buttons, ornaments, or coasters*

Oriental Trading Co., Inc.
4206 South 108th Street
Omaha, NE 68137
402-331-6800
800-228-2269

*An extensive line of toys, novelties, balloons, seasonal items*

Sherman Specialty Co., Inc.
114 Church Street
Freeport, NY 11520
516-546-7400
800-645-6513
800-669-7437

*Activity books, placemats, crayons, meal pails, toys, stickers, and balloons*

Table Toys™ Inc.
2500 Central Parkway, Suite P
Houston, TX 77092
713-956-9900
800-999-8990

*Primary colored, 29" × 29" table surface with interlocking building blocks designed to keep children occupied before or after eating*

U.S. Toy Company, Inc.
1227 East 119th Street
Grandview, MO 64030
816-761-5900
800-255-6124

*Full line of constructive playthings, with marketing planning guide available*

Zoo Piks International
1190 Explorer Drive
Duncanville, TX 75137
214-298-8444
800-321-7667

*Wide range of drink picks and ice trays in shapes ranging from teddy bears to dinosaurs*

## VENDING

Giant Gumball Machine Co., Inc.
200 Meyers Road
Grand Prairie, TX 75050-4739
214-262-2234
800-634-2855

*Large-capacity, 79" tall, 42" in diameter gumball machine*

Kiddie Rides International
5500 Greenwood Plaza Boulevard
Suite 274
Englewood, CO 80111
303-721-8910
800-448-6888

*The largest manufacturer and importer of kiddie rides in the United States, with 70 different rides available*

The Robot Factory
P.O. Box 112
Cascade, CO 80809
719-687-6208

*Remote, radio-controlled talking robots in a variety of appearances, performing a variety of functions*

# Index